ICON OF AN AGE

TITANIC

ICON OF AN AGE

TITANIC

MICHAEL McCAUGHAN

BLACKSTAFF PRESS
BELFAST
in association with
NATIONAL MUSEUMS
NORTHERN IRELAND

AUTHOR'S ACKNOWLEDGEMENTS
For encouragement and help in preparing this book my best thanks are due to family and former museum colleagues. I also want to express my appreciation to Blackstaff Press for their editorial dedication and commitment to high production values. Finally my warmest gratitude to Yvonne for her unflagging support and forbearance, as always.

∞∞

First published in 1998 as *The Birth of the Titanic*

This edition published, with additional material, in 2012 by
Blackstaff Press
4c Heron Wharf, Sydenham Business Park
Belfast BT3 9LE
in association with
National Museums Northern Ireland
Cultra, Holywood,
Co. Down, BT18 0EU

© Photographs and other illustrations copyright of National Museums Northern Ireland
Every effort has been made to trace and contact copyright holders before publication. Any errors or omissions will be rectified, upon notification, at the earliest opportunity.
All rights reserved

Where known, reference numbers are given alongside images, except for p.58: 'Gold star' OMAFP-2012-27-82; 'Second class views' OMAFP-2012-27-310; 'White Star flag' OMAFP-2010-27-123

Michael McCaughan has asserted his right under the Copyright, Designs and Patents Act 1988 to be identified as the author of this work.

Typeset and designed by Two Associates

Printed in Italy by Sedit

A CIP catalogue record for this book is available from the British Library

ISBN 978-0-85640-865-6

www.blackstaffpress.com
www.nmni.com

National Museums Northern Ireland
explore/engage/enjoy

for Yvonne, Fionola, Peter, Aaron and Cait

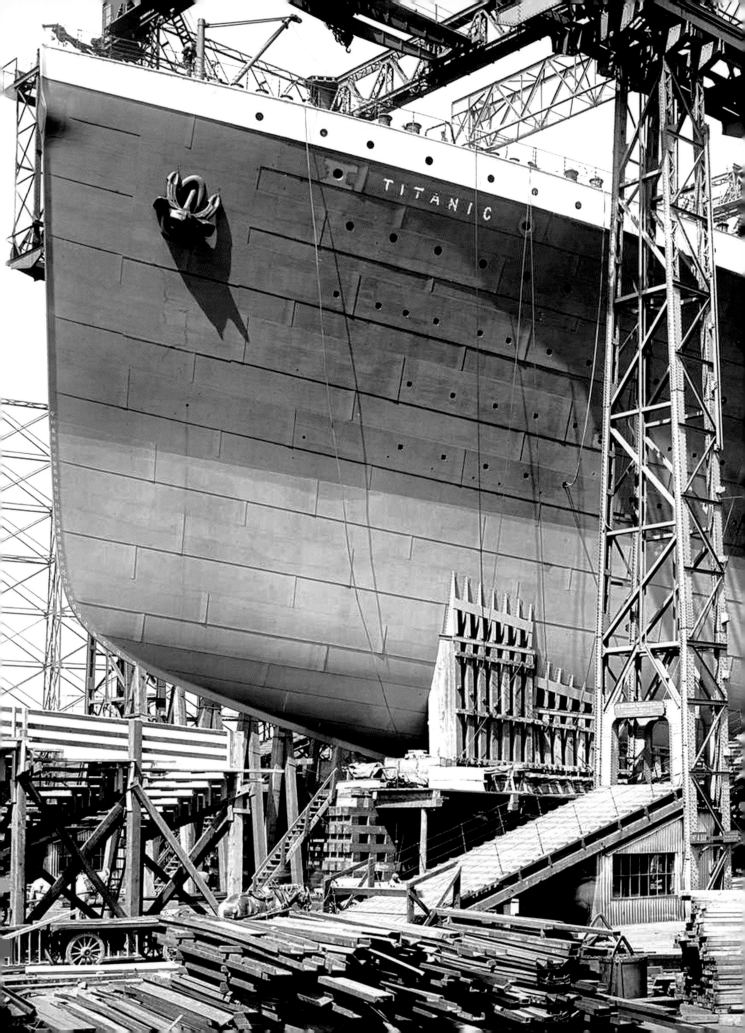

CONTENTS

Introduction 8

1: A *Titanic* World 14

2: *Titanic*'s Homeland 26

3: A Great Shipbuilding Tradition 34

4: The White Star Line 58

5: *Titanic* Conceived 72

6: The Yard Prepares 84

7: Building the Hull 100

8: Launch Day 122

9: Behind the Scenes 134

10: Fitting Out 148

11: Accommodation 174

12: Leaving Belfast 198

13: Embarkation 206

14: 'We Are on the Ice' 222

Photographs and Photographers 244

⟨ *Titanic*'s hull in
readiness for launch
day, 31 May 1911.
(H1561)

TITANIC is the most famous ship in history. Her story is one of the epic tales of the twentieth century. On the evening of 14 April 1912, *Titanic* – the essence of modernity and technological achievement – was steaming across the Atlantic on her maiden voyage from the Old World to the New. All on board – from wealthy capitalists to stateless emigrants, the ship's officers and her labouring crew – were oblivious to the iceberg's presence and the imminence of destruction and death. Enshrining the values, self-confidence and social fabric of the era, *Titanic* was a microcosm of western civilisation and its misplaced certainties in a 'gilded age' before the First World War. The spirit of the times was reflected and proclaimed, with unknowing irony, in the White Star Line's grandiloquent advertising of *Titanic* and her sister ship *Olympic*.

OMAFP-2010-27-632

The *Olympic* and *Titanic* are not only the largest vessels in the World; they represent the highest attainments in Naval Architecture and Marine Engineering; they stand for the pre-eminence of the Anglo-Saxon race on the Ocean ... The White Star Liners *Olympic* and *Titanic* – eloquent testimonies to the progress of mankind, as shown in the conquest of mind over matter – will rank high in the achievements of the twentieth century.

When *Titanic* struck the iceberg her steel hull was opened below the waterline for a length of 300 feet. The inrush of water, with which the pumps and system of hull subdivision could not cope, doomed the ship. There were not enough lifeboats to save all of the 2,201 people on board. There was provision for only 1,178 people, but not even all of the available lifeboats were filled to capacity. Boats were lowered only partly filled with passengers who refused at first to believe that *Titanic* could possibly sink. More than 1,500 people, passengers and crew, lost their lives in the freezing waters of the Atlantic. The sinking of *Titanic* had a traumatic effect in both Europe and the United States. The great ship, a signifier of the civilised world, now lay fractured on the ocean floor after plunging down through two miles of freezing water. Millionaires and emigrant poor had gone down with her. It was a mighty blow to the self-confidence of the age. An American writer, Bruce Jackson, has interpreted the impact of the disaster from a modern perspective:

OMAFP-2010-27-130

The rising star of modern technology had a sudden loss of magnitude, as that sleek and enormous ship that could not be sunk tore its hide and collapsed. It was the major disaster of the era, and it struck the imagination of the rich, who lost friends and relatives on the ship ... and the poor, for whom the ship represented the great shining and glistening world forever denied them and anyone they would ever know.

For many in 1912, the wreck of *Titanic* was rich in symbolic significance. Her sinking called into question the established order of things. It deeply troubled those who implicitly believed in a good and merciful God. For others, the disaster was widely regarded as a fateful warning, or confirmed their belief in divine retribution for conceit and arrogance. It seemed to demonstrate the folly of human presumption and the vanity of the belief that nature could be conquered by science. The Bishop of Winchester preached:

When has such a mighty lesson against our confidence and trust in power, machinery and money been shot through the nation? The *Titanic*, name and thing, will stand for a monument and warning to human presumption.

The destruction of *Titanic* by a spur of ice shattered popular faith in the supremacy of technology, progress and privilege. The age of self-confident belief in the inexorable progress of society through the appliance of science was over.

Throughout the twentieth century, and now, well into the twenty-first, *Titanic*, and all that her loss implies, has maintained a powerful hold on the imagination of people, not only in Europe and North America, but virtually throughout the world. Potent images of the stricken liner have endured for decades, while the multiplicity of metaphors resulting from the catastrophe has been equally powerful. Cultural processes of absorption, transformation and diffusion began immediately after the sinking and, as resonances of *Titanic*'s disaster, they perhaps have significance for humanity greater than the event itself.

Titanic and the mythic proportions of her loss have become the subject, generator and carrier of all kinds of signs, messages and meanings, from the sublime to the tacky. They embrace the cultural spectrum, from high culture to low culture, and from popular culture to consumer culture. *Titanic*, or rather Titanicism, is an international cultural phenomenon which shows no sign of abating. Despite the magnitude of other horrors, *Titanic* has achieved the status of ultimate disaster symbol in our cultural consciousness. *Titanic*, both real

Titanic (left) and *Olympic* together in Belfast for the last time. The photograph was taken on 6 March 1912 to record a difficult operation to exchange the positions of *Titanic* and *Olympic* on the tide, vis-à-vis the deepwater wharf and the drydock. *Titanic* was temporarily removed from the wharf to the drydock in order to provide more space to swing *Olympic* in the narrow channel, following her removal from the drydock after propeller repairs. In the photograph *Olympic* is lying at the deepwater fitting-out wharf temporarily vacated by *Titanic*, while *Titanic* herself is being manoeuvred into the nearby drydock. The operation was carried out under the direction of Thomas Andrews and Charles Payne of Harland & Wolff, while Captain Bartlet, marine superintendent of the White Star Line, was on board *Titanic* and Commander Smith was on the bridge of *Olympic*. (L4122/2)

and imagined, has become a key icon of popular culture and one of the great metaphors of our time.

The cultural abstractions of Titanicism contrast with the human reality of the catastrophe in which over 1,500 souls perished in the most appalling circumstances imaginable. The essential tragedy of *Titanic* was not the loss of the ship itself, but the huge loss of life because there were insufficient lifeboats for all on board. Yet with the passage of time attitudes to the disaster have changed and for us today *Titanic* has a significance beyond tragedy and death.

Nevertheless, while *Titanic* belongs to the past, it is not yet the distant past where archaeologists feel safe. In a way the iconic *Titanic* is in limbo or a time warp between the present and the past. For many the *Titanic* disaster is not quite history, but an event still connected to the present by resonating chords of memory. This is particularly so in the north of Ireland, for Belfast was the birthplace of *Titanic* and there remains a thwarted pride in the unfulfilled achievement of the great lost ship.

Titanic is now a worldwide brand fusing profit, pleasure and memorialisation. In her homeland she has become an important signifier and agent of economic, social and cultural regeneration. Of course, the emblematic *Titanic* is the carrier of a complex of messages and meanings. Today in Belfast the ship's metaphorical status is multi-dimensional and allows for the existence of different kinds of *Titanic* – from the real to the reconstructed, from the remembered to the imaginary and from substance to pastiche. Yet the core symbolism of the *Titanic* disaster remains. Essentially the cataclysmic sinking of *Titanic* is a paradigm for the inevitable failure of flaunted technology, the fragility of human ambition, the shipwreck of dreams and the transience of life.

⌄ At the end of May 1911 *Titanic* was ready for launching. This photograph shows the enormous scale of the steel hull, together with the complex structure of the enfolding gantry, from which she will soon be free. The photograph also reflects old and new maritime technologies – the traditional wooden schooner in the foreground contrasting with the modernity of *Titanic*, which represented 'the highest attainments in Naval Architecture and Marine Engineering'. (WAG 3734)

It is the birth and building of *Titanic* in Belfast which is the core theme of this book. Essentially it is a chronicle of historic photographs, illustrations and interpretative text which combine to provide unique insights into and perspectives on *Titanic* and her times. The White Star leviathan is placed in the wider context of the Edwardian era and industrial Belfast, together with shipbuilding at the Queen's Island works of Harland & Wolff Ltd, which then was the largest shipyard in the world. In addition, *Titanic* and shipyard production are set against contrasting themes of tradition and modernity in the northern Irish province of Ulster around the 1912 period.

Olympic in drydock, April 1911. In selecting this ⟩ dramatic viewpoint directly below the bows of the ship, the photographer, R.J. Welch, unknowingly prefigures *Titanic*'s hull seconds before her fatal collision with the iceberg. (H1506)

H1506
R.W.

1

A TITANIC
WORLD

I N a speech reported in *The Times* newspaper on 24 May 1909, Winston Churchill declared:

> We have arrived at a new time. Let us realise it. And with that new time, strange methods, huge forces, larger combinations – a Titanic world – have sprung up around us.

In creating this potent image of the emerging modern world, Churchill unconsciously anticipated the resonating name of the great doomed liner which, in life and death, was so emblematic of the Edwardian age. Even as he addressed his Manchester audience, construction of *Titanic* was beginning in Belfast – where her keel had been laid on 31 March 1909 – as Harland and Wolff's Ship No. 401.

In 1901 it seemed that the start of the new century represented some kind of pattern shift in the complex fabric of society. Queen Victoria's long reign had ended and her son, Edward VII, had succeeded to the throne. The country had entered the Edwardian age, a period that in essence would continue beyond the death of Edward in 1910, into the early years of George V's reign, and end with the Great War in 1914. It was an age characterised in part by continuing advances in science, medicine and technology, including electrical engineering.

As innovative transportation technology, the electrification of London's underground had led the way in the 1890s and now the new electric tramways signified modernity and progress in the cities of Britain and Ireland, with Belfast's system opening in 1905. But the voltage power of electricity was no longer restricted to travel, or the generation of light: it was to become wired to an enormous range of appliances and systems, from the domestic to the industrial. In department

∧ Power to the vacuum cleaner: advertisement, May 1912

∧ Sausages take to the skies: advertisement, December 1911

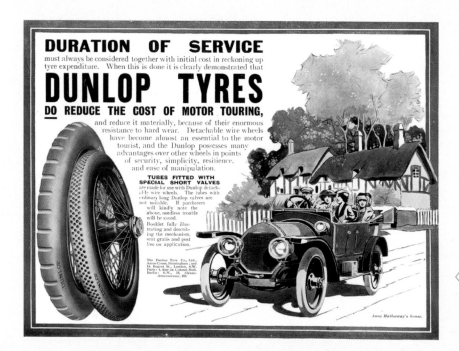

Tyres for motoring tourists: advertisement, April 1912

stores electric motors drove escalators and lifts to carry customers from floor to floor, and by the end of the period, new retail electrical goods, such as smoothing irons and vacuum cleaners, had come on to the market, together with electric model train sets and Marconi-type wireless transmitters – an extraordinary range of merchandise was now available to the nation.

Advances in consumerism, transport and communications technology brought direct economic benefits to Edwardian society. With increasing leisure time and disposable incomes, there were also exciting possibilities for transport-related recreational activities, especially motoring. The motor car became the new and desirable high-tech status symbol, initiating an extensive motor manufacturing and supply industry, including a thriving trade in the sale of motoring accessories and in fashionable ranges of protective clothing for open-air driving. The thrilling new skill of driving, often at speed, appealed to women as well as men, encouraging competitive racing and leading to the rise of international motor sport. All this was due to the development of the internal combustion engine, which, as the radical prime mover of the age, also brought about significant advances in marine propulsion and made possible the revolutionary development of powered flight.

Within a short time of the American Wright brothers' first powered flight in 1903, daring aviators, exposed to the elements in their wood and fabric flying machines, were taking to the skies over Britain and France. Fundamentally it was the development of lightweight internal combustion petrol aero engines that made extended powered flight possible. By 1909 Louis Bleriot had flown across the English Channel and at the end of the same year Ulsterman Harry Ferguson, later of tractor fame, made the first powered flight in Ireland in his self-built monoplane. In 1910 Lilian Bland, also from Ulster, became the first woman in the world to build and fly her own aircraft.

∨ Distinguished partakers of
tonic wine: advertisement,
April 1912

Signing their Declaration of Confidence in
SANATOGEN
The Tonic Food

FREE SAMPLE.

SANATOGEN

On the water, the marine internal combustion engine established leisure motorboating as a popular pastime, while coastal fishing boats began to make the transition from sail to motor power, as various designs of engines using paraffin or oil fuel became available. Across the North Sea in Germany, Rudolf Diesel was developing an oil-fuel compression-ignition internal combustion engine, to which he gave his name, and which later proved so reliable in the U-boats of the First World War. Although still in the pioneering stages of development as a weapon of war, all naval submarines of the day were products of advanced new technologies, using internal combustion engines for surface propulsion and battery-powered electric motors when submerged.

However, while electric motors and combustion engines were new power systems, they had not replaced the steam engine as the dominant prime mover in industry, manufacturing and transport. For generations, coal-fired boilers had powered various designs of reciprocating steam engines on land and sea in every sphere, from mills and factories to railways and shipping. Over the years advances in marine engineering were particularly significant. With improved boilers, pressures were increased and steam was expanded, first through two-engine cylinders and then three-engine cylinders, to achieve greater efficiency and economy. By the late nineteenth century the triple-expansion marine engine had become the standard propelling machinery at sea, with the triple-expansion engines of *Titanic* and her sister ships being the largest ever built.

During the Edwardian period marine reciprocating machinery reached its final development with complex quadruple-expansion engines being installed in a number of ships. Some of these engines were built by the Belfast shipyard of Workman Clark, Harland and Wolff's great rival across the River Lagan. This firm also was a pioneer in the building of steam turbine machinery, the revolutionary high-speed steam propulsion system invented by Charles Parsons. Turbine machinery, fast and compact, was quickly adopted by the Royal Navy, together with oil-fired boilers, for its new generation of super-battleships, beginning with HMS *Dreadnought* in 1906. Characterised by rotary rather than reciprocating motion, turbines were also fitted in Cunard's 1907 high-speed, 27-knot, record-breaking liners *Mauretania* and *Lusitania*, to which the White Star Line responded with the larger and even more luxurious *Olympic* and *Titanic*. The huge reciprocating machinery in *Titanic* was combined with a massive low-pressure steam turbine which, like the twin main engines, was the largest of its kind, driving the ship at a speed of over 22 knots.

Along with these technological advances, the Edwardian period is popularly regarded as a happy golden age of peace, order and settled tranquillity. Reflecting the increasing wealth and aspirations of the middle classes, it enjoyed the practical pleasures of early modernity. However, the Edwardian age was also characterised by pressures for significant social, economic and political changes. Many of these had their roots in the previous century, but now they had come to the fore and were in tension with an established capitalist hierarchy of essentially male conservative conventions and interests. As the early years of the twentieth century unfolded, the complexities, contradictions and diversities of a wealthy but unequal society became apparent. In stressful ways, not hitherto experienced, opposing patterns of continuity and change, innovation and tradition, security and anxiety, and complacency and foreboding raised questions and challenged long-established comfortable assumptions.

This was a time fraught with discontent and demands for greater equality between the prosperous and the poor, the privileged and the exploited, and, even more radically, the ending of inequality between the sexes. Consequently the character of the age was in part shaped by the Suffragette campaign for women's voting rights. Significant changes were taking place in the relationships between men and women, predominantly those in the middle classes. The new feminists – active at the forefront of society, in every area from political activism to pioneering aviation – created anxieties and insecurities for some men, whose dominant male virility seemed under threat. At the same time, however, while some women were striving for greater freedoms, many others were being ever-more bodily constricted by new corset technology designed to achieve the hourglass figure so desired by fashionable women.

Cocoa for women workers: advertisement, December 1906.

THIS . . .
WOMAN WORKER
is one of the many typists, lady clerks, dressmakers, &c., who have to work incessantly under very unfavourable conditions, but who by taking the simple precaution of having a cup of Vi-Cocoa before going out to work in the morning and after returning at night, are enabled to perform their daily work with a sense of pleasure and satisfaction.

Vi-Cocoa affects beneficially both the old and the young, and possesses property equally valuable to the weary brain worker and to the man or woman whose labours are more particularly manual.

When you go to your grocer's be sure and order a packet of Vi-Cocoa. No test is so good as the actual test in your own home. One packet will prove our claims and you will join the great army of Vi-Cocoa users. Why not get a packet now? Your grocer has it ready for you.

DR TIBBLES' Vi-Cocoa

If this was indeed a Golden Age, it shone most brightly on the leisured and prosperous upper and middle classes. There was a somewhat duller glow for the working class, whose living conditions had improved, but for those in poverty – and there were many – the gilded age passed them by. For the poor, the emancipation of women and their demands for greater equality in society had little relevance.

The character of the age was in part shaped by workers striking for improvements in wages and working conditions, together with the complementary rise of organised labour through the trade union movement and the newly formed Labour Party. There were reforms in public health, the regulation of child labour and the raising of safety standards in factories. Recognising the needs of those too old to work, in January 1909 the Liberal government also introduced the first Old Age Pension for men and women over seventy years of age.

Along with the social and economic turmoil at home, there also came latent fears and forebodings about the future of the Empire itself. In the nineteenth century Britain had been the first industrial state – the workshop of the world – but now its economic dominance and manufacturing capacity were being overtaken by the United States and Germany. The increasing rivalry of the German Empire was worrying, not only because of commercial competition and the development of a new German merchant marine, but particularly because its rapidly expanding imperial High Sea Fleet was seen as a challenge to the supremacy of the Royal Navy on which Britain's maritime power, empire and overseas wealth depended. The Kaiser's declaration, 'Our future lies on the water', directly threatened Britain's naval might and mercantile marine. Inevitably it resulted in huge naval shipbuilding programmes in Britain and Germany – a powerful naval armaments race of increasing momentum which locked the two empires directly on to a collision course, culminating in the Great War.

Within three years of Churchill's 'Titanic world' speech, the great ship that was the embodiment of this world would meet its end. The conclusion of the inquiry into the sinking of *Titanic* in 1912 was that it 'was due to collision with an iceberg, brought about by the excessive speed at which the ship was being navigated.' In other words, over-confident reckless driving at speed in the dark had caused *Titanic*'s iceberg crash. The unsinkable microcosm of the age had experienced a sudden and mortal failure of progress. Speeding to disaster was an unnerving extension of Churchill's 'Titanic world' metaphor, for speed was the defining characteristic of Edwardian Britain: speed of the new, speed of change, speed of machines, speed on land, speed in the air, speed on water and speed into the unknown.

A German patriotic postcard reflecting national pride in the Kaiser's development of maritime power. Wilhelm II wears an admiral's uniform as head of the Imperial Navy. The top of the card is emblazoned with the Kaiser's declaration of German naval expansion, translated as 'Our future lies on the water'. The personal message written on the postcard shows that it was sent from the spa town of Wiesbaden by an English visitor in December 1900.

‹ Racing car No. 6 competing in the 1903 international Gordon Bennett Trophy Race on a circuit of closed public roads around Athy in Co. Kildare. Early motor racing was a dangerous sport and this Irish event, with teams from Europe and America, was the first major motor race to be held in the United Kingdom. Car No. 6, a streamlined Belgian-built Mors, was one of the French team's racers and had a top speed of over 80 m.p.h. It was driven by 23-year-old Fernand Gabriel, the youngest competitor, who finished in fourth place. The Mors was right-hand drive, so in the photograph Gabriel is seen on the left, with his mechanic in the passenger seat. There was strong Irish support for the French team, which achieved second, third and fourth places in its blue-painted racing machines. The return to Dublin of one of the French cars is the setting for James Joyce's short story 'After the Race' from *Dubliners* (1914).

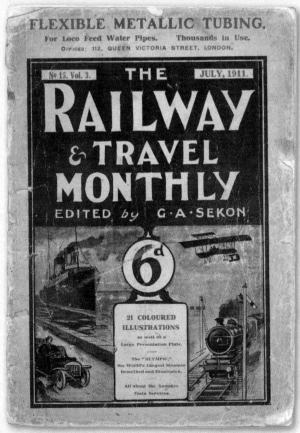

‹ Front cover of *The Railway and Travel Monthly*, July 1911, depicting modern means of transport by sea, road, rail and air. This issue of the magazine carried a special feature, with colour illustrations, on the new White Star liner *Olympic*. (OMAFP-2010-27-451)

THE PRICE OF SPEED

Many old arguments have been revived by the appalling disaster to the " Titanic." The general conclusion is that we are travelling too fast. Traffic accidents by sea and land are not new, however, and hard facts show that modern travel becomes more safe year by year. We can only judge these matters by comparing accidents with the total mileage travelled, and on this basis it is evident that modern modes of transit are safer than the older methods. We pay a high price for speed, however, and we should be willing to learn when an occasional disaster proves how far off we still are from perfection.

Like the motor car and the bicycle, the aeroplane was a product of the modern industrial age. The first powered flight in Ireland took place on 31 December 1909 in Hillsborough, Co. Down. The pilot was Harry Ferguson, pioneer aviator and subsequently inventor of the famous Ferguson tractor system. This photograph was taken in 1911, with the young Ferguson precariously perched in the cockpit of the linen-covered aeroplane he had built himself. His mechanic is holding the tailplane, while young women spectators watch from a distance. (L860-1)

Post-*Titanic* disaster reflection on the price of speed, published in *The Sphere*, 27 April 1912. It headed a regular feature by R.P. Hearne called 'In the Petrol World: Leaves from an Observer's Notebook'.

Advances in corset design: advertisement,
August 1909

In the struggle for votes for women, shocking scenes
of the force-feeding of suffragette prisoners on
hunger strike helped win support for the cause. This
disturbing poster shows the roles played by male
doctors and a woman warder in the forcible feeding
of the helpless female prisoner through a nasal tube.

In April 1912, a 25-year-old American aviator,
Harriet Quimby, became the first woman to
fly across the English Channel, following
Frenchman Louis Bleriot's pioneering flight
in 1909. She piloted a similar monoplane
aircraft but, unlike Bleriot, she flew from
England to France, climbing to a height of
2,000 feet. In reporting Harriet Quimby's
achievement, *The Sphere* magazine placed
pictorial emphasis on her leather-clad
appearance as a pilot, contrasting it with
her clothing before and after the flight.

On 31 August 1910, Lilian Bland, a pioneering aviator from Carnmoney near Belfast, became the first woman in the world to build and then fly her own aircraft. An independent young woman who worked as a journalist, she had experimented with her own design of glider before fitting it with a 20-horsepower aero-engine brought from England. In the photograph, Lilian Bland is at the controls of her biplane *Mayfly*, with the engine and 'pusher' propeller mounted behind the seat. She had plans to build and sell her aircraft to order. However, in the spring of 1911, Lilian's father, concerned about the dangers of flying, persuaded her to give up her aviation activities by offering to buy her a motor car instead. After taking on a Ford car sub-agency in Belfast, she married and then emigrated to Canada.

Intrepid balloonist Mrs John Dunville was a member of the wealthy Dunville whiskey family of Holywood, Co. Down. She featured in the 1910 Christmas edition of the Irish women's magazine *The Lady of the House*. Described as a distinguished Irish lady aeronaut, Mrs Dunville was photographed in her husband's balloon *Banshee,* in which they had together crossed the English Channel. The balloon, with a capacity of 80,000 cubic feet, was inflated alongside the local gasometer.

2
TITANIC'S HOMELAND

BELFAST, with a population of 386,947 in 1911, was a commercial and industrial city unlike any other in Ireland. As a major port exporting to world markets, its wealth was keyed to shipbuilding, engineering, manufacturing and the production of linen. Belfast's modernity was reflected, for example, in its extensive electric tram system connecting the city centre with ever-growing suburbs. The new City Hall, opened in 1906, was a marbled temple to civic pride. Its municipal grandeur contrasted with the stark industrial skyline of Harland & Wolff's shipyard, dominated by the great steel gantry where, from 1909, *Titanic* was taking shape.

Outwardly Belfast projected self-confident progress, the achievement of which was premised on capitalist enterprise and control of a large labour market. Nevertheless, tensions and strains were discernible in the economic, social and political fabric of the city. Labour unrest was mounting, unemployment was increasing and trade unions were mobilising. While the middle-class suburbs developed rapidly, there was a fall in the

∧ Castle Junction, Belfast *c.*1912. In this city of commercial prosperity, the bustle and traffic of the busy streets have been frozen in time. Representing modernity and progress, the electric trams in the main thoroughfare of Royal Avenue seem to bear down on a horse-drawn wagon and jaunting car. The Bank Buildings, on the corner of Castle Street, were home to one of Belfast's large new department stores. Completed in 1900, it was the city's first modem steel-frame building. (WAG 3789)

Postcards of the Belfast Dock Strike in 1907 were published in the city. Here the Labour leaders are addressing strikers at Queen's Square. From the left they are Messrs McKeown, Boyd, Larkin, Murray and McKessock (standing).

numbers of houses built for the working classes. In general, the gap between the rich and the poor was widening, as the latter's standard of living declined.

Demands for better wages and improved working conditions, especially for unskilled casual workers, came to a head in the summer of 1907 with a widespread strike and lockout known as the Belfast Dock Strike. It was a major industrial crisis affecting the whole city, with 4,600 dockers and carters receiving mass working-class support from both Catholic nationalists and Protestant unionists. The strike was led by the charismatic socialist James Larkin of the National Union of Dock Labourers and by Alex Boyd, organiser of the Municipal Employees Association. Despite sackings, blackleg labour and lockouts, the strike was a pioneer mobilisation of labour which brought Belfast to a standstill. Troops were drafted in to support the police, some of whom had also gone on strike. Riots and shootings in early August led to British trade union leaders bypassing Larkin to negotiate a settlement with employers. The strike ended on 28 August with an agreed pay increase for workers and the right of employers to take on non-union labour. However, the socialist unity forged between Catholics and Protestants by the strike was short-lived and in the Home Rule crisis of 1912–14 old sectarian divisions would re-emerge.

Outside the urban centres of Belfast and the city of Derry, the northern province of Ulster was characterised by an economy based on agriculture and rural industries. It was a landscape of scattered farms and market towns, with fishing and other maritime activities on the coast. However, in the early decades of the century there were signs that traditional country life was changing. The increasing availability of manufactured consumer goods gave impetus to a transition from an older culture to a society more dependent on modern technologies and factory-made products. Nevertheless, the pace of change was uneven and for many people, especially in remote districts, everyday life remained rooted in the past.

Overall, despite accelerating change and the advent of modern times, aspects of traditional rural society remained deeply embedded in the consciousness of the population, not just in the countryside, but also to a surprising extent in the towns and cities of Ulster.

In 1912, the Liberal government in London, with the support of Irish nationalist MPs, had been in the process of setting legislation which would establish devolved government for Ireland – Home Rule. Unionist Ulster was in political turmoil. The unionist captains of industry and commerce, and the Protestant working class, felt threatened by this rise of Irish nationalism and the prospect of Home Rule for Ireland, which they were determined to resist. Between 1912 and 1914 the crisis deepened as unionists formed the paramilitary Ulster Volunteer Force, paradoxically to oppose Home Rule by armed insurrection against the British government in order to remain part of the United Kingdom.

In this highly-charged political atmosphere, there were sectarian assaults on Catholic shipyard workers, and the belief spread among many Catholics that the *Titanic* had enshrined anti-Catholic messages, such as the alleged ship number '3909 ON', a mirror image of the sectarian slogan 'No Pope' (*Titanic*'s actual ship number was 401). Inevitably, the creation and destruction of *Titanic* became a popular text which reflected the political, religious and sectarian tensions fissuring Ireland in the Home Rule crisis of that time. With fearful symmetry, *Titanic* sailed on her maiden voyage the day before the third Irish Home Rule Bill was introduced in the House of Commons on 11 April 1912.

Postcard of an anti-Home Rule demonstration in Belfast on 8 February 1912 to protest against a visit by Winston Churchill MP. As a member of the Liberal Government and First Lord of the Admiralty, he had come to speak at a pro-Home Rule meeting organised by the Ulster Liberal Association. In Royal Avenue, in the city centre, Churchill was met by crowds of noisy and hostile demonstrators, including shipyard workers. In the photograph, the destination of the tram is Queen's Road – the main thoroughfare of Queen's Island – and so it is likely that these particular protesters have come from the shipyard.

'Of all the cities and towns in Ireland, Belfast has the least interest in any history before the Act of Union. She is enormously occupied with her present, enormously and justly proud of what her citizens are and of what they have accomplished. But what should most concern all Ulstermen and all Irishmen is the future of Belfast – for with it is inextricably bound up, for good or for evil, the whole future of the Irish nation.'
Stephen Gwynne, *The Famous Cities of Ireland*, 1915

In the north of Ireland large numbers of postcards were produced depicting unionist resistance to Home Rule and an embattled determination to remain British. Characteristically defiant and pugnacious, the cards were designed as pictorial propaganda to mobilise unionist sentiment in Ulster and gain support in Britain for the unionist cause.

Popular nationalistic postcards often included depictions of Ireland's Celtic Revival. They romantically drew on Ireland's ancient Gaelic past, with the national symbols of shamrock and harp as recurring motifs in green and gold. On this card, lyrical lines from Thomas Moore's 'Irish Melodies' chime with nationalist anticipation of Home Rule and Irish freedom.

Pattern makers' > workshop in Belfast City Tramway's Sandy Row depot in 1906. The system was electrified in 1905 and the model of Tram No. 1 was made in the workshops the following year. The model was used for training tram-men and to illustrate public lectures on Belfast's extensive tramway system. (WAG 3167)

Ireland's large railway > network was important to the economic and social life of the country. Narrow-gauge railways were built to serve the more remote districts. Here, at Ballycastle in Co. Antrim c.1914, the passenger train almost ready to leave the station is headed by *Countess of Antrim*, a locomotive built in 1880. (WAG 835)

A Co. Donegal fisherman prepares to launch his currach in Sheephaven Bay *c*.1915. Because of its lightweight construction and tarred-canvas covering, piers and harbours are not essential for its use. Formerly skin-covered, the currach belongs to an ancient European boatbuilding tradition which has survived on the Atlantic coast of western Ireland. (WAG 255)

While *Titanic* was being built in industrial Belfast, ancient forms of transport were still in use in the countryside. In the remote Glens of Antrim, the wheel-less slide car, drawn by a mountain pony, survived as a working vehicle until well into the twentieth century. (WAG 270)

Harvest time on a farm near Toome, Co. Antrim *c*.1914, with labour-saving machinery co-existing with manual work. In a significant division of labour, men are operating the horse-drawn reaper while the women bend to tie the fallen corn into sheaves before they are stacked into stooks for drying. (WAG 1158)

3

A GREAT
SHIPBUILDING
TRADITION

THE shipbuilding industry was firmly established in Belfast in 1791, when William Ritchie began the construction of wooden sailing ships. Other builders followed, but it was not until the second half of the nineteenth century that Belfast became world-renowned for the construction of first iron and then steel ships. Technologically, the building of iron hulls was not an extension of wooden shipbuilding, but rather a development of the expanding ironworking industry of boilermaking. Significantly the first iron vessel built in Belfast was constructed by the engineering and boilermaking firm of Victor Coates & Co., who launched a Lough Neagh steamer, *Countess of Caledon*, in 1838.

Queen's Island, Belfast.

⟨ Postcard showing shipyard gantries and ships under construction, with steam tugs in the foreground.

In 1853 the Belfast Harbour Commissioners laid out a shipyard on Queen's Island for Robert Hickson, a partner in a local ironworks. However, Hickson was not so much a shipbuilding visionary as a businessman seeking an outlet for his iron boilerplating. He had little ability as a practical shipbuilder and in 1854 he appointed a young Yorkshireman, Edward James Harland, as his yard manager. Four years later Hickson sold the business to Harland for £5,000, and in 1861 it became known as Harland & Wolff when Gustav W. Wolff joined Harland as a partner in the new firm.

From their formation Harland & Wolff established a reputation for constructing high-quality ships designed to suit an owner's particular requirements. Furthermore, their ships frequently combined advanced technology with innovative naval architecture. For example, during the 1860s, the firm's entirely new concepts in iron-ship design provided hull strength and additional cargo capacity without increase in engine size and hence without increase in fuel consumption. After 1880 Harland & Wolff made significant advances in steam engine design and, in the twentieth century, in diesel and turbo-electric machinery.

As shipbuilders with a large output of passenger vessels, the company pioneered improvements in the quality of accommodation in all classes, most notably in ships built for the White Star Line. Harland & Wolff also developed the capacity to build ships of huge dimensions, although in later years these were tankers and bulk carriers rather than passenger liners.

Today, however, Harland & Wolff no longer builds ships. Their last ship, the 20,000-ton *Anvil Point* (Ship No. 1742), was completed in 2003 but the company remains a major ship repairer, with sophisticated engineering and fabrication facilities. Now known as Harland and Wolff Heavy Industries, it provides a broad range of services to marine industries, including offshore wind farms and the development of wave power generators.

∨ In the 1890s and early 1900s, Harland & Wolff underwent considerable expansion as the demand for ships grew. The scale of the Queen's Island works is suggested in this elevated view of the North Yard in June 1906. Smoke and steam billow from the workshops and sheds in the foreground while in the background Ship No. 358, *Adriatic*, is under construction on Slip No. 3, with its overhead gantry and surrounding mass of timber staging. (H980)

In nineteenth-century Belfast, the development of iron shipbuilding was not confined to the yard of Harland & Wolff. Victor Coates & Co. continued in business until the 1860s, and about 1868 the firm of MacIlwaine & Lewis added shipbuilding to their engineering and boilermaking works at Abercorn Basin. In 1886 they took one of the new shipyards laid out by the Belfast Harbour Commissioners and were in operation until 1894, when, as MacIlwaine & MacColl Ltd, they were taken over by Workman Clark & Co.

The firm of Workman Clark & Co. was registered in April 1880. Their first ship, the steam coaster *Ethel*, was launched in August 1880 to the order of A. McMullin of Ballymena, Co. Antrim. The compound steam engine for the ship was supplied by the Belfast engineering firm of J. Rowan & Sons, as Workman Clark's engine works were not built until 1891. From about 1900 Workman Clark became specialist shipbuilders, as Harland & Wolff had been from their inception. Their yard pioneered, for example, the development of the refrigerated steamship and in 1904 built the *Victorian* as the first transatlantic turbine-powered passenger liner. In terms of output the company, in 1902, was at the top of the list of world shipbuilders with a total gross tonnage of 86,712. Prosperity declined, however, after the First World War and Workman Clark & Co. finally went out of business in 1935, with Ship No. 536 being their final yard number.

Despite the necessity to import iron and steel, the raw components of shipbuilding, there were a number of factors, in addition to business enterprise, which favoured the growth of shipbuilding in Belfast. The city is at the end of a sheltered deep-water lough to which shipyards had easy access after the completion of the Victoria Channel in 1849. Not only was there ample space for expansion on the reclaimed slobland of Queen's Island, but the excavation of drydocks was also relatively easy, thus keeping down costs. No comparable site for expansion existed in the north of Ireland outside Belfast, although iron shipbuilding was also located in Derry, together with smaller yards in Larne and Carrickfergus.

By separating trade and shipbuilding activities in the port, the Belfast Harbour Commissioners avoided the situation that occurred on the Mersey, where the development of the docks and quays constricted shipbuilding. Furthermore, they actively encouraged the growth of this important industry by laying out small yards on Queen's Island and building larger drydocks as the size of ships increased. These far-sighted policies of the Harbour Commissioners were a crucial factor in the successful development of the shipbuilding industry in Belfast.

Cabinetmakers at work in Harland & Wolff's cabinet shop in 1899. With shipyard production geared to the building of passenger liners, large numbers of skilled craftsmen and journeymen were employed in the ship outfitting trades. Huge quantities of wooden furnishings and fittings were needed for the cabins and public rooms of a large liner, so the efficient organisation of production in the cabinet shop was particularly important. The bowler-hatted figure in the foreground is probably the shop foreman. (H545)

Efficient business administration was an essential part of the shipbuilding enterprise at Queen's Island. Here clerks are hard at work in Harland & Wolff's counting house in the main office block on Queen's Road. The photograph, taken about 1903, reveals interesting details, such as the electric desk lights and the claw-hammer coat worn by the chief clerk sitting at the right-hand desk. Like the shipyard as a whole, this office was a male preserve. (H605A)

⟨ When *Olympic* and *Titanic* were built, Harland & Wolff was the largest and one of the most modern shipyards in the world. In this 1912 photograph of the hull-drawing office, smartly dressed naval architects and draughtsmen are working on ship designs. The high barrel ceiling of the office and the large number of windows make maximum use of natural light. (H501)

⋏ Hull drawings were scaled up in the mould loft. In this photograph, taken *c*.1910, three loftsmen are chalking the lines of a ship on portable wooden flooring, full size for cross-section and quarter scale for length, in order to determine the precise shapes needed for the ship's steel frames. The floor-to-ceiling windows again maximise natural light, while the timber Belfast truss roof, a common feature of shipyard workshops and sheds, combines a large span with relatively low weight. (H57)

In 1896 Harland & Wolff began a massive reorganisation of the shipyard. This followed a disastrous fire, coupled with the need to provide the necessary facilities for the construction of a huge new White Star liner. In 1899 the re-equipped yard was extensively photographed by R.J. Welch. His photographs include this unusual view of the painters' studio, with white-jacketed painters working on embossed panels for the interior decoration of a passenger ship. The numerous large windows and overhead glazing provided a high level of natural light, augmented as necessary by electric and gas lights suspended from the timber roof. (H505)

This 1899 view of the painters' shop and its practical messiness contrasts with the neatly ordered atmosphere of the painters' studio. Paint was mixed in the rows of wooden barrels and decanted into small pots for the painters. Paint powder can be seen on the right of the photograph, while in the background there is a belt-driven device for tumbling the paint barrels, together with a tank of turpentine and a row of fire buckets for emergencies. (H506)

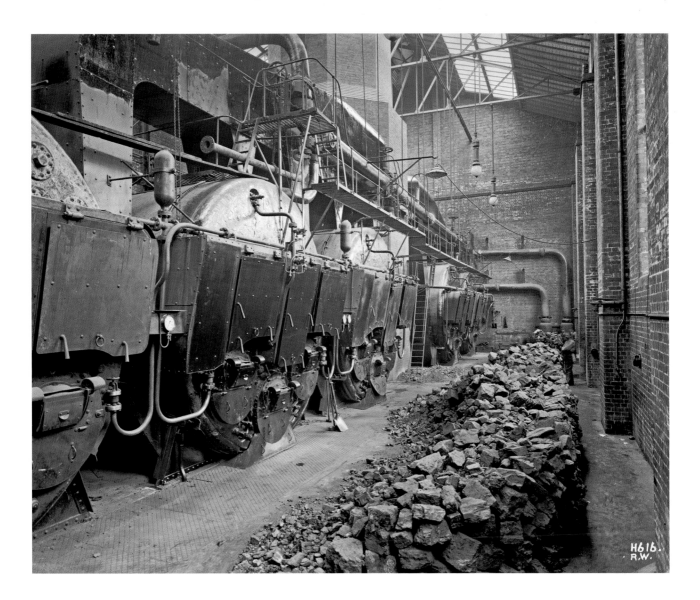

Interior of Harland & Wolff's generating station in 1912 after the installation of oil-fuel gas engines. In this clinically clean building, the engines and linked generators provided the electrical current needed for tools, machinery and lighting throughout the shipyard. The original steam-powered generating station was commissioned on 24 October 1904, replacing the supply of electrical current from Belfast Corporation. (H614)

The pristine condition of the generating station contrasts with the coal dust and grime of the steam boiler house, photographed in 1912. Here coal was constantly shovelled into the furnaces of the boilers to maintain steam pressure for the generating engines. Although the working conditions were hot and filthy, they were rather better than those endured by stokers in the boiler rooms of *Titanic*. (H616)

The hull of a ship under construction was a skeletal structure of immense strength. Internal steel frames acted as ribs, while the external skin or shell plating made the vessel watertight. Here shipyard workers pose for the photographer in front of the newly erected stern frames of Ship No. 317, *Oceanic*, on 3 November 1897. The complex curvature of the massive frames will allow the later fitting of propeller shafts, while the surrounding web of timber staging both supports and contrasts with the steel skeleton of the ship. (H38)

When launched on 4 April 1901, Ship No. 335, *Celtic*, was the largest ship in the world at 20,904 tons. In the photograph men on the slip are beginning to clear the ways, which have been lubricated with tallow and soft soap, in preparation for laying the keel of the next ship. On the water, men in a scow are recovering launch debris, while tugs prepare to manoeuvre *Celtic* to the fitting-out wharf for completion. (H698)

Launch party on the platform immediately before the naming ceremony of Ship No. 342, *Walmer Castle*, on 6 July 1901. This was one of a series of successful mail steamers built by Harland & Wolff for the South African service, first of the Union Line, then the Union-Castle Line. In the photograph W.J. Pirrie, chairman of Harland & Wolff, is third from the right. Standing next to him is the white-bearded Sir Donald Currie, chairman of the Union-Castle Line. G.W. Wolff, now an elderly man, is fifth from the left, wearing a white hat. A ribboned bottle is ready to be smashed against the looming steel hull of the 12,545-ton ship as part of the naming and launching ceremony. (H712)

∧ The elegant splendour of first-class
accommodation in a great Edwardian
liner is reflected in this view of the ladies'
reading room on board the White Star liner
Adriatic. Completed in April 1907 as Ship
No. 358, *Adriatic* was the immediate White
Star forerunner of *Olympic* and *Titanic*.
At 24,540 tons, she was one of the largest
ships in the world and inaugurated the
Line's new service from Southampton to
New York. With a maximum speed of 18
knots and a crew of 557, *Adriatic* carried
425 first-class passengers in luxurious
comfort. (H1001)

∧ Second-class library of the *Adriatic*, April
1907. Accommodation in passenger ships
was often described as first for luxury,
second for comfort and third for economy.
Adriatic could carry up to 500 second-class
passengers in considerable comfort. Note
the swivel chairs bolted to the deck while
one of the ship's masts, passing through the
library, is grained to match the decor of the
room. (H1122)

H1125
R.W.

Third-class dining saloon of the *Adriatic*. The ship was designed to carry 1,900 passengers in the third or emigrant class, as against 500 in second class and 425 in first class. The 'emigrant trade' was a very profitable business for transatlantic shipping lines and thousands crossed to the New World in accommodation such as this. Although White Star's Belfast-built ships were noted for the quality of their accommodation, third-class passengers still were fed in relays in this austere and functional dining saloon. Nevertheless, it was a great improvement on the conditions endured by earlier generations of emigrants. (H1125)

As a shipbuilding firm competing in world markets, Harland & Wolff built passenger liners for a number of European shipping companies. The Holland–America Line was a particularly important customer and Ship No. 390, *Rotterdam*, was a significant order for Harland & Wolff. When completed in June 1908, the interior of the 23,980-ton liner was photographed extensively. Unusually, the views included this photograph of the first-class pantry, with its tea- and coffee-making facilities, together with silver-service teapots, entrée trays, toast racks and rows of jugs hooked overhead. (H1304)

Panoramic view of the port of Belfast, May 1911, showing the busy docks (lower foreground) and across Victoria Channel to Harland & Wolff's enormous shipyard at Queen's Island. Beneath the steelwork of the great gantry (right), *Titanic* is almost ready for launching, while at the deepwater wharf (far left) *Olympic* is nearing completion. (1262)

THE MEN OF THE SHIPYARD

Shipbuilding was a male-dominated, labour-intensive industry employing a wide range of skilled, semi-skilled and unskilled workers. The enormous variety of tradesmen needed to build a ship included riveters, riggers, fitters, shipwrights, platers, caulkers, drillers, smiths, mechanics, carpenters, cabinetmakers, coppersmiths, plumbers and painters, besides redleaders, cementers and general labourers. Wages, often based on piece work, varied considerably but the top earners were the skilled craftsmen who had served apprenticeships and were members of trade unions. They could earn £2 a week or more, whereas an unskilled labourer might take home less than £1. Shipyard men worked from 6 a.m. to 5.30 p.m. five days a week and a half day on Saturday. The shipbuilding labour force was predominantly Protestant but significant numbers of Catholics were also employed. Shipyard workers lived in different areas of the city but there was a particular concentration in Protestant east Belfast, close to Queen's Island.

Portrait photographs of shipyard men are unusual. In this carefully composed group photograph, dozens of shipyard workers gaze out from a century ago. Although their names and the lives they led are unknown, they have been memorialised in this photograph against the black hull of Titanic.

Shipyard workers pose for a group photograph during construction of the White Star liner *Adriatic* in 1906. Beyond their life in the yard, the 'Islandmen' enjoyed various hobbies and interests, from breeding terriers and poultry, to whippet racing, politics, literature and the natural sciences. The man on the far right of this photograph, Robert Bell, was a keen amateur geologist and mineralist who discovered several species of fossil mollusca, which were subsequently named after him. (H978)

Crowds of shipyard men leaving Queen's Island at the end of a working day in May 1911. Some of them have boarded electric trams bound for parts of the city beyond walking distance. In the foreground a barefoot boy is selling newspapers, while in the background *Titanic* looms, under her huge gantry, almost ready for launching. In this period Harland & Wolff employed about 15,000 men. Between 3,000 and 4,000 of them were engaged in the completion of *Titanic*. (H1555A)

Steel-plating the ship's hull began when all the frames and crossbeams were in place. Here a squad of men is operating a hydraulic riveter on the topside shell plating of the *Oceanic* on 1 October 1898. The whole structure of the ship is held or pinned together by thousands of steel rivets, the domed heads of which can be clearly seen in the photograph. For the construction of *Oceanic*, the hard physical work of hand-riveting had been partially mechanised by the introduction of faster, labour-saving hydraulic riveters, suspended from the overhead gantry. Nevertheless, dozens of hand-riveting squads were still required for working on parts of the hull inaccessible to this powerful new device. (H160)

H160

WHITE STAR LINE

ROYAL AND UNITED STATES
MAIL STEAMERS
LIVERPOOL · NEW YORK
LIVERPOOL · BOSTON
NEW YORK · MEDITERRANEAN
BOSTON · MEDITERRANEAN

WHITE STAR LINE SOUVENIR

WHITE STAR LINE.

AMERICAN SERVICES

BOOKLET OF SECOND CLASS VIEWS

WHITE STAR LINE
ROYAL & STEAMERS
UNITED STATES MAIL

M.S. "OCEANIC,"
LIVERPOOL TO NEW YORK,
WEDNESDAY, JUNE 17th, 1903.

Contract Ticket No. 2 1125

INSPECTION CARD.
(Immigrants and Steerage Passengers.)

Port of Departure, LIVERPOOL.

Name of Ship "OCEANIC"

Name of Immigrant *Wahlberg Gustaf*

Date of Departure, 2nd November

Last Residence *Saleborg*

Inspected and passed at	Passed at Quarantine, port of	Passed by Immigration Bureau,
NEW YORK NOV 10	U.S.	port of
	(Date.)	(Date.)

INFORMATION F
OCEAN TRAVEL

CONTAINING PARTICU
OF THE

AMERICAN
ATLANTIC TRANSPO
DOMINION
LEYLAND
RED STAR
AND
WHITE STAR

THE
WHITE STAR
LINE

WITH the end of the American Civil War in 1865, there was a marked rise in the number of people crossing the Atlantic in both directions –from emigrants bound for the New World and travelling businessmen, to American socialites and tourists visiting Europe. The prospect of large profits to be made from this increasing volume of transatlantic passenger traffic led directly to the formation in 1869 of the White Star Line – more formally known as the Oceanic Steam Navigation Company Ltd, Liverpool. It was to be in direct competition with the Cunard, Inman, Guion and National steamship lines, companies already established in the lucrative North Atlantic passenger trade.

Emigrants departing from Queenstown.   Co. Cork.

∧ Queenstown, now Cobh, in south west Ireland was the final port of call for liners crossing the Atlantic. They anchored offshore while the mails and passengers, mainly emigrants, were ferried out on steam tenders. For thousands of Irish people, Queenstown was a place of parting and departure – the sad leaving of family and friends to seek a new life in America.
(OMAFP-2010-27-146)

The original capital of the White Star Line was £400,000, comprised of four hundred £1,000 shares, fifty thousand of which were held by its founder, Thomas H. Ismay. Other investors in the enterprise were active in the shipping trade of Liverpool, including the Belfast shipyard principals, Edward J. Harland and Gustav W. Wolff.

Oceanic, the pioneer steamship of the White Star Line, was completed in 1871 by Harland & Wolff, Belfast, and set new standards of accommodation and naval architecture. Designed by Edward Harland, the most innovative shipbuilder of the day, *Oceanic* exemplified a radical new style of fast transatlantic liner. She was characterised by a long narrow iron hull with a straight stem and the revolutionary positioning of the first-class accommodation amidships. This kept first-class passengers away from propeller vibration in the stern and reduced the effects of pitching in heavy weather.

Built to outclass all her rivals, *Oceanic* was quickly followed by five close sister ships in 1871–72. From the beginning, passenger comfort was the keynote feature of White Star ships. In each of these vessels, improved amenities included large cabins, more headroom, better ventilation, water taps, and, in the public rooms, marble fireplaces and a piano, together with swivelling wooden armchairs in the dining saloon.

The success of *Oceanic* initiated a close business relationship between owners and builders that would be

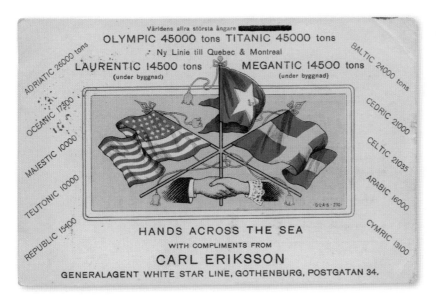

Rare *Titanic* and *Olympic* promotional card for White Star's Swedish shipping agent Carl Eriksson. It reflects the international make-up of passengers sailing in *Titanic* and other liners. Names of ships in the White Star fleet surround the central panel. The motif of hands clasped across the sea was popular with emigrants and those left at home. (OMAFP-2010-27-181)

maintained until the demise of the White Star Line following its merger with Cunard in the mid-1930s. With one exception, all White Star vessels prior to the First World War were built by Harland & Wolff, and many of these ships, usually designed and built in series, marked significant advances in the development of the North Atlantic passenger liner. So intimate were the social and business links between the companies that Harland & Wolff were usually free to build White Star ships to their own specifications and without cost limitations. On completion a fixed percentage was added to the total expenditure and this constituted their construction fee. This unique business arrangement, known as 'cost plus', lasted for over sixty years and the building of some sixty ships for the line.

Within three years of the completion of the original six White Star ships, another pair of larger and more advanced liners – *Britannic* and *Germanic* – joined the fleet. *Germanic*, a famous record-breaker, cut the transatlantic crossing time to just over seven and a half days. Both ships remained in company service until 1903.

During the 1880s, with no new tonnage, White Star ships began to be eclipsed by rival Cunard and Inman liners. To remain competitive, in 1889–90 White Star brought out *Teutonic* and *Majestic* as a pair of radically new greyhounds of the ocean. Built of steel rather than iron, each was powered by two triple expansion engines driving twin propellers, which made the carrying of sails no longer necessary. With raked masts and tall twin funnels, these innovative ships introduced a modern profile to the Atlantic liner. While *Teutonic* and *Majestic* were technically advanced record-breakers, they

White Star advertisement, in a marine Art Nouveau style, promoting the Line's various transatlantic services and global shipping interests. (OMAFP-2010-27-79)

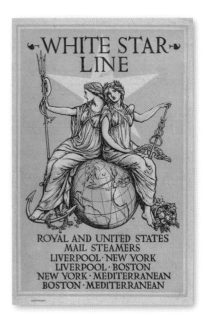

also incorporated major improvements in passenger accommodation in all classes, from electric lights to lavatory facilities. The first-class public rooms and staterooms were richly appointed in high Victorian fashion, promoting a sense of superlative luxury at sea.

The huge building costs of these ships were offset by an Admiralty contract to convert them, if necessary, to armed merchant cruisers mounting naval guns. On completion, and with guns fitted, *Teutonic* took part in the Spithead Naval Review of 1889, displaying her status as the world's first armed merchant cruiser. This aspect of *Teutonic* was of particular interest to the young Kaiser Wilhelm when he toured the ship with the Prince of Wales. The Kaiser's close inspection of *Teutonic* helped reinforce his ideas for expanding the German merchant marine and Imperial Navy as rivals to British maritime power.

By the late 1890s, with rapid developments in the size, speed and accommodation of premier Atlantic liners, *Teutonic* and *Majestic* were outclassed by new German and Cunard ships. White Star's competitive response was to build, in 1899, another *Oceanic* as the largest and most luxurious ship in the world, with an emphasis on steadiness rather than outright speed. Advances in ship design over the last thirty years of the century were reflected in the tonnage differences between the first *Oceanic* of 1871, at 3,707 tons, and the second *Oceanic* of 1899, at 17,274 tons. The new *Oceanic* was a liner of exceptional elegance, with a striking profile dominated by two huge funnels. She had accommodation for around 400 in first class, 300 in second class and 1,000 in third class. Such was the success and popularity of *Oceanic* that White Star no longer focused on record breaking but concentrated instead on luxury, comfort and great size with moderate high speed. Essentially *Oceanic* initiated a business strategy which led to the building of *Olympic* and *Titanic* in the following decade.

In 1902 the White Star Line became a constituent company of a huge international shipping combine known as the International Mercantile Marine Company (IMM). Formed that same year by the American financier, J. Pierpoint Morgan, the aim of IMM was to gain control of the major shipping lines in the North Atlantic trade and thereby achieve

⌃ Lord Pirrie, chairman of Harland & Wolff Ltd. His autocratic management style often terrified his staff, but he was a consummate international businessman.

⌃ Bruce Ismay, chairman and managing director of the White Star Line. He sailed on *Titanic*'s maiden voyage and survived the disaster.

∧ Private office of Harland & Wolff's chairman Lord Pirrie, at Queen's Island, Belfast *c*.1912. Under Pirrie's
leadership Harland & Wolff became the most powerful shipbuilding enterprise in the world. As chairman,
Pirrie forged business alliances and controlled the central accounts of the company, while the managing
directors were given responsibility for production, cost control and labour relations. (H503)

a rate-fixing monopoly. Following the acquisition of a number of important companies,
Morgan made a successful takeover bid for the prestigious White Star Line. The accepted
offer was in excess of £10,000,000, and in December 1902 the company passed out of British
control. However it was agreed that Bruce Ismay, son of the founder of the Line, would
remain as managing director and company chairman, and that the ships, though principally
American-owned, would retain their British registry and continue to be manned by British
officers and crews.

The White Star Line became a subsidiary of the International Navigation Co. Ltd of
Liverpool, which in turn was owned by IMM, registered in New Jersey. Eight of the thirteen
directors controlling the combine were American, while the five British directors included
Bruce Ismay and W.J. Pirrie, chairman of Harland & Wolff Ltd, and also a director of the
White Star Line.

In 1904 Ismay became president of IMM and with unlimited powers he attempted to
improve its financial and administrative structure. He was supported by Pirrie, whose aim
was to promote Harland & Wolff as shipbuilders to the constituent lines of the combine,
in addition to continuing the special relationship with White Star. It was White Star's
absorption into IMM, with resultant access to large capital resources, that ultimately made
possible the construction of *Titanic* and her sister ships *Olympic* and *Britannic*.

Shipping agent's notice for the steamship lines of the International Mercantile Marine Company. The White Star Line was a constituent company of this American shipping combine from 1902 to 1927. (OMAFP-2010-27-32)

Rare White Star prepaid steerage ticket receipt for a family of Irish emigrants sailing from Queenstown to New York in 1879. It details their names, ages and cost of the ticket ($112). Patrick and Catherine Foley with their young children James and Mary were accompanied by Michael Murphy, probably Catherine's father. Interestingly the ticket was purchased by a John Murphy, possibly Michael's brother. (OMAFP-2010-27-97)

FILE THIS.
WHITE STAR LINE
UNITED STATES AND ROYAL
Mail Steamers.

TEUTONIC arrived at 6.12 A. M. yesterday; with Saloon and Second Cabin passengers only. Passage 5 days, 21 hours and 8 minutes. She sails at 3 P. M. on October 5th, with Saloon, Second Cabin and Steerage passengers as usual. Second Cabin, $40 and $45.

MAJESTIC arrived at Queenstown at 1 A. M. on Wednesday morning.

NOTICE.

To AGENTS :—

On receipt of this you will please discontinue the sale of Outward Tickets to all German, Belgian, Dutch and French Ports—but you may continue the sale of tickets to Scandinavian and Finnish Ports. This cancels the clause in our postal of the 23rd inst. authorizing booking to Bremen and Rotterdam.

SPECIAL NOTICE.

I regret that it is necessary to decline issuing tickets in favor of Russians or Poles, **to any point** and agents will therefore until further notice refuse to sell a ticket to any Russian or Pole. This regulation must be strictly enforced.

H. MAITLAND KERSEY, Agent.
New York, Sept. 29, 1892.

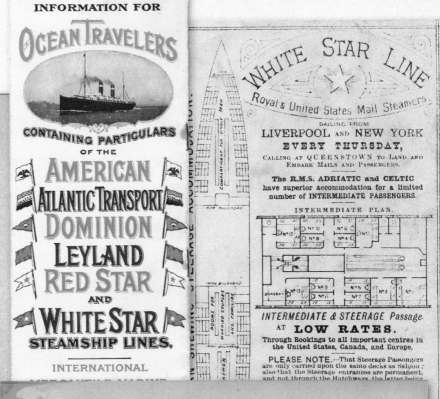

INFORMATION FOR
OCEAN TRAVELERS
CONTAINING PARTICULARS
OF THE
AMERICAN
ATLANTIC TRANSPORT
DOMINION
LEYLAND
RED STAR
AND
WHITE STAR
STEAMSHIP LINES.
INTERNATIONAL

WHITE STAR LINE
Royal & United States Mail Steamers.
SAILING FROM
LIVERPOOL AND NEW YORK
EVERY THURSDAY,
CALLING AT QUEENSTOWN TO LAND AND
EMBARK MAILS AND PASSENGERS.

The R.M.S. ADRIATIC and CELTIC have superior accommodation for a limited number of INTERMEDIATE PASSENGERS.

INTERMEDIATE PLAN.

INTERMEDIATE & STEERAGE Passage.
AT **LOW RATES.**
Through Bookings to all important centres in the United States, Canada, and Europe.

PLEASE NOTE.—That Steerage Passengers are only carried upon the same decks as Saloon ; also that the Steerage entrances are permanent, and not through the Hatchways, the latter being

---

WHITE STAR LINE.
Special Notice to Passengers

...s respectfully requested that Passengers refrain ...hrowing into the pan any substance likely to ... the pipes, or prevent a proper flow of water ; ...se serious discomfort to the Passengers them- ...may be caused, and the closet rendered both ...eable and useless.   Passengers are earnestly ... to flush the pan before leaving.

FILE THIS.
WHITE STAR LINE.
NEW YORK, September 2, 1892.
SPECIAL NOTICE.

The President of the United States, having issued a proclamation, imposing a quarantine of twenty days against all vessels **from any foreign port** carrying immigrants. Agents are hereby notified that the WHITE STAR LINE, will discontinue carrying steerage passengers from Liverpool and Queenstown until further notice.

H. MAITLAND KERSEY, AGENT.

CAUTION !

Several robberies having lately occurred in the Staterooms of various European Steamers, before leaving the wharf in New York, the Managers of the WHITE STAR LINE request passengers to be careful in leaving their baggage only in charge of the Company's servants, and that money, jewelry, or other valuables be given in care of the purser, who will issue a receipt, and deposit the articles in the ship's safe.

The White Star Line issued a wide range of notices to passengers and the company's agents, together with informational advertisements to attract transatlantic travellers. (*Clockwise from top left*: OMAFP-2010-27-100; OMAFP-2010-27-462; OMAFP-2010-27-124; OMAFP-2010-27-138; OMAFP-2010-27-316; OMAFP-2010-27-162)

OCEANIC, 1871

S.Walters. · *Steam Ship "OCEANIC" White Star Line.* Registered.

White Star promotional card for *Oceanic*, the Line's first steamship built in 1871. It was reproduced from an original painting by the Liverpool marine artist Samuel Walters. He depicts the long clean lines of *Oceanic* with her straight stem and raked masts. Like other liners of the time, she had a single propeller and so sails were carried for use in the event of a breakdown. Sails were also set in favourable winds to assist the relatively low engine power and help minimise coal consumption. (OMAFP-2010-27-183)

' The long and intimate relations of the two firms form one of the most interesting chapters in the history of our shipbuilding industry. They have led the way, the one in British mercantile marine enterprise, the other in shipbuilding progress – to their mutual benefit, no doubt, but also to the benefit and progress of Belfast. Our shipbuilding stands where it does in the shipbuilding of the United Kingdom largely owing to the connection between the two firms established by their founders, and maintained in such relations by their present respective heads, Lord Pirrie and Mr Bruce Ismay. And its position is unchallengably at the top of the mercantile marine.'
Belfast News-Letter, 21 October 1910

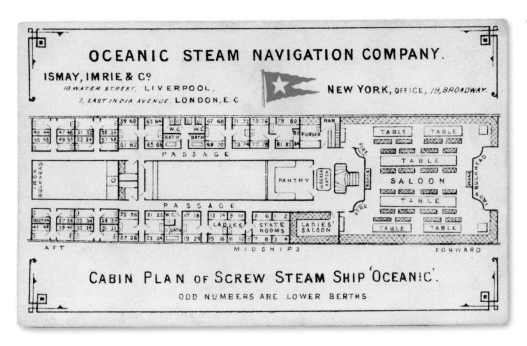

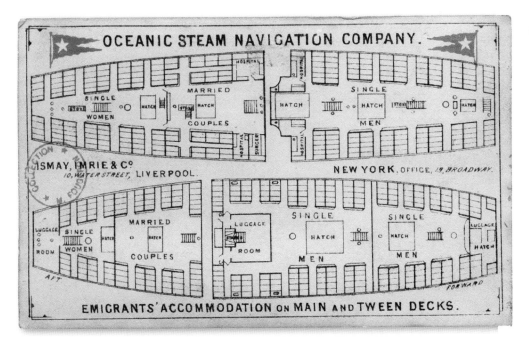

With their first ship the White Star Line, or Oceanic Steam Navigation Company, introduced the revolutionary positioning of first class accommodation amidships rather than at the after end of the ship as was customary in other liners. This first class cabin plan shows iron bulkheads fore and aft, which were a safety feature and helped isolate first class from other passengers. Note the piano placed against the forward bulkhead. (OMAFP-2010-27-1823)

The new *Oceanic* offered improved standards of accommodation for emigrants on two decks. Dormitory style berths were divided into areas for single women, married couples and single men, the last group forming the largest category. (OMAFP-2010-27-182)

TEUTONIC, 1889

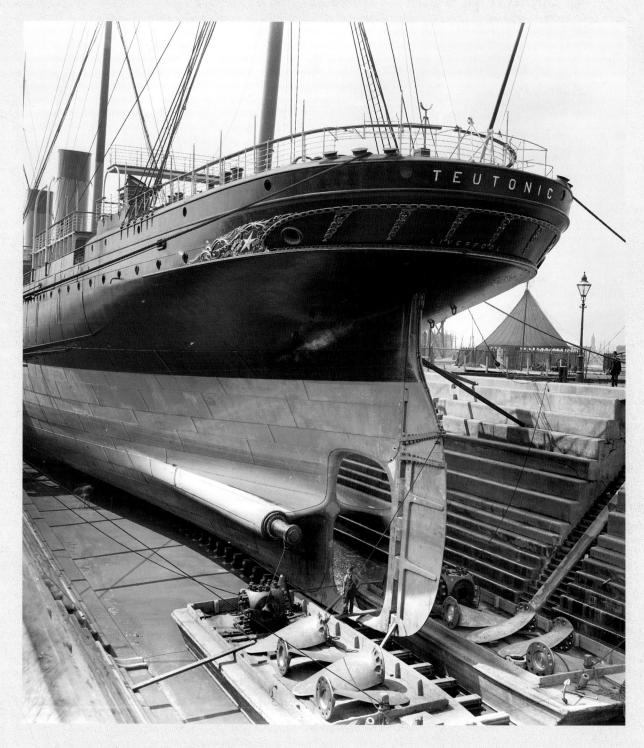

White Star's innovative liner *Teutonic* nearing completion in 1889 in the Belfast Harbour Commissioners' new Alexandra Graving Dock. Designed as the first twin screw liner for the North Atlantic, *Teutonic*'s propeller blades are ready to be bolted on to the propeller shafts. As a twin screw ship, *Teutonic* no longer carried sails. (H2123)

H.I.M. The Emperor of Germany
and
H.R.H. The Prince of Wales
inspecting the
"TEUTONIC"
at Spithead on August 4th 1889.

⟨ As the world's first armed merchant cruiser in the event of war, *Teutonic* sailed from Belfast to the Naval Review at Spithead in August 1889. Her deck guns were of particular interest to the Kaiser, but they were removed before the ship went into service as a White Star passenger liner. (OMAFP-2010-27-372)

⌄ Guests of the White Star Line on board *Teutonic* at the Spithead Naval Review, 26 June 1897, which commemorated Queen Victoria's Diamond Jubilee. Deck guns were fitted for the occasion in keeping with her naval role as an armed merchant cruiser in the event of war. (*Teutonic*, 056)

OCEANIC, 1899

A SPECIAL TRAIN leaves EUSTON STATION, London, at 12 o'clock, noon, on day of Sailing, conveying Passengers and their Baggage direct to RIVERSIDE STATION.

WHITE STAR LINE
ROYAL & STEAMERS
UNITED STATES MAIL

R.M.S. "OCEANIC,"
LIVERPOOL TO NEW YORK,
WEDNESDAY, JUNE 17th, 1903.

FIRST CLASS PASSENGERS
Will embark with their Baggage at the PRINCE'S LANDING STAGE on WEDNESDAY, the 17th JUNE, not later than **5** p.m. :

BAGGAGE.—Passengers are requested to see that their Baggage is distinctly labelled for Hold or Stateroom, and heavy packages consigned to our care for shipment should be sent with advice of despatch, at least three days before sailing.

To prevent disappointment, Passengers are respectfully informed that Packages of Merchandise will not be allowed to be shipped as Luggage. Any excess of Luggage over Twenty Cubic Feet measurement will be charged Freight.

First Class Passengers embarking at Queenstown must be at that Port not later than 10-15 a.m. on Thursday, 18th June.

ISMAY, IMRIE & CO.,
30, JAMES STREET, LIVERPOOL;
17, Cockspur Street, S.W., and 34, Leadenhall Street, E.C., LONDON.

650—4/6/03

Aldridge 73

This is a particularly dramatic view of the *Oceanic* on the stocks in preparation for her launch on 14 January 1899. Built for the White Star Line, she was designed to be the largest and most luxurious ship of the nineteenth century, with a registered length of 685.7 feet and measuring 17,274 gross tons. Her construction, which entailed the erection of a new overhead gantry and a general expansion of shipyard facilities, was a notable achievement for Harland & Wolff. The importance of *Oceanic* is indicated by her hull being painted light grey to aid photography. Before launching, the heavy timber shores would be removed, but the timber cradle supporting the ship's bows would remain in place. The steel plates in the foreground are stacked vertically for ease of handling. (H186)

White Star publication promoting the Line's new flagship *Oceanic*, which entered service in 1899. With an elegant profile dominated by two huge funnels and tall raked masts, *Oceanic* set new standards of accommodation in transatlantic travel. In this depiction her arrival on the ocean is greeted by Neptune bearing the White Star houseflag. (OMAFP-2010-27-419)

At Ellis Island in New York harbour, European immigrants and steerage passengers were subject to medical inspections before being allowed to land in the United States. This Inspection Card, stamped 10 November 1904, shows that Swedish immigrant Gustaf Wahlberg crossed from Liverpool in the White Star liner *Oceanic*, which had accommodation for 1,000 steerage passengers. As the Inspection Card is unpunched and stamped 'S' denoting senility, it is likely that Mr Wahlberg was refused entry to the US and returned to Sweden. (OMAFP-2010-27-84)

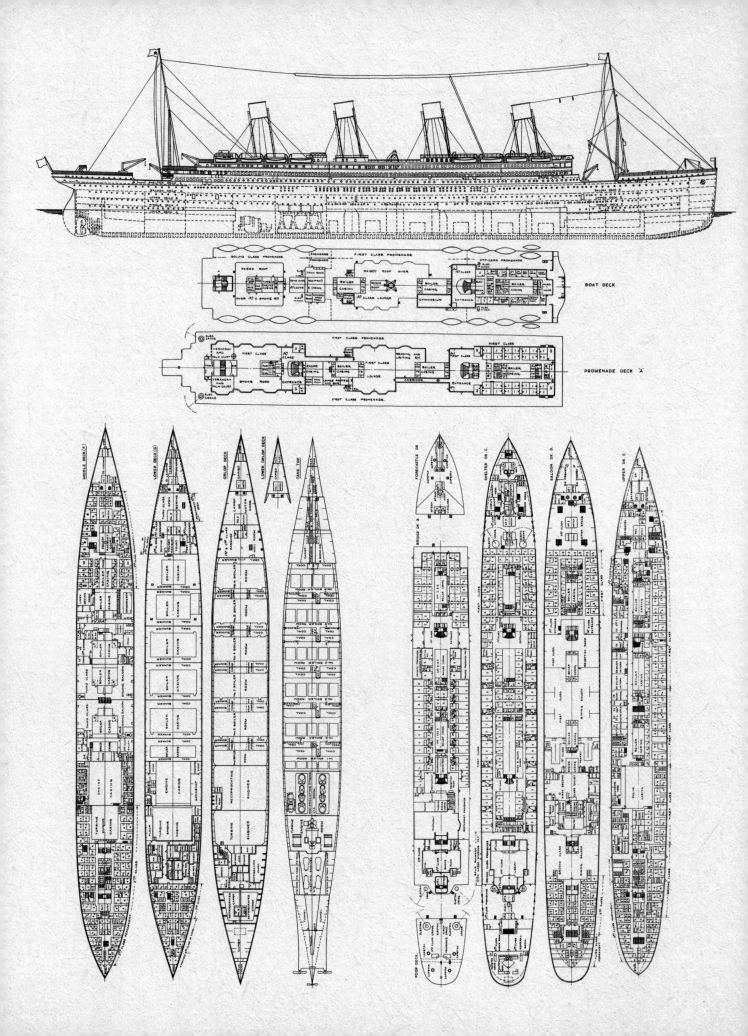

5

TITANIC
CONCEIVED

CONTRARY to popular belief, *Titanic* was not a unique one-off ship, but was the second of an intended trio of huge passenger vessels for the White Star Line's premier service between Southampton and New York. *Titanic* (1912) and her sister ships *Olympic* (1911) and *Britannic* (1914) were conceived as the company's response to increasing competition on the North Atlantic, particularly from Cunard's express turbine liners *Mauretania* and *Lusitania*, which were the largest, fastest and most luxurious ships in the world when built in 1907.

White Star's competing strategy was to build three leviathans half as big again, with even higher standards of accommodation in all classes and designed overall as the embodiment of dignity and elegance at sea. First-class passengers, especially wealthy Americans, were to be seduced to the new White Star ships, not by the promise of very high-speed crossings as offered by the rival Cunarders, but by the prospect of travelling in supreme luxury and steadiness on the ocean at moderately fast speed in the largest vessels afloat.

The construction of these enormous ships by Harland & Wolff at Queen's Island, Belfast, was a considerable technological achievement, with each succeeding vessel being of increased tonnage and improved design. As the pioneer ship of the trio, *Olympic*, 45,324 gross tons, was the chief focus of attention at the time, and the subject of considerable discussion in both the popular and technical press.

In contrast, there was much less contemporary publicity for the construction and entry into service of *Titanic*, as the new ship was a virtual replica of *Olympic*. However, she did incorporate a number of improvements in the arrangement and decoration of the first-class passenger accommodation. Additional enclosed space, notably in the size of deck houses, resulted in *Titanic* having a larger, gross tonnage of 46,328, although hull dimensions of the two ships were almost identical. Externally *Titanic* was distinguished by the partial enclosure of the promenade deck, which on *Olympic* was entirely open.

The third sister ship, *Britannic*, 48,158 gross tons, was not launched until February 1914 and was fitting out at Queen's Island when the First World War began the following August. She was taken over by the government and completed as a hospital ship on Admiralty orders.

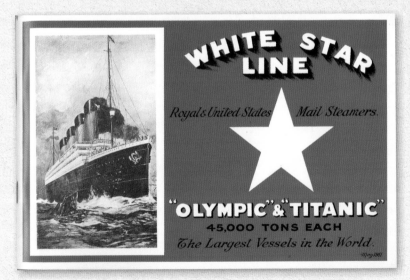

∧ Cover of White Star booklet describing
Olympic and *Titanic*, May 1911

Britannic was commissioned in 1915, but on 21 November 1916 she struck a mine in the Aegean Sea and sank within an hour. She never entered the liner service for which she was designed, and of the three great ships only *Olympic* survived to be a commercial success, carrying passengers on the North Atlantic until 1935, when she was sold for breaking-up, following the Cunard/White Star merger and subsequent rationalisation of the new company's fleet.

∧ Cover of White Star booklet marking the launch of *Britannic*. (TR 62-4)

‘The science of shipbuilding ... has now reached to a degree of perfection in its highest form which has put wind and water almost at defiance. It has not only robbed the sea of its terrors, but it has imposed upon its unstable surface comforts, and even luxuries, of travel surpassing anything on land. Those who cross the continents of the deep today in the latest triumphs of the science of marine architecture have all the conveniences, all the comforts, and all the luxuries that can be commanded on shore. The story of the accommodation of a great ocean liner would have read like a fairy tale to the last generation.’ *Belfast News-Letter*, 21 October 1910

THOMAS ANDREWS

Thomas Andrews was Harland & Wolff's chief designer, a nephew of the chairman, Lord Pirrie, and a managing director of the company. His gentlemanly personality and profession of practical shipbuilder are projected in this informal portrait of Andrews *c.*1911 in his rather crumpled working suit with upturning lapels. He had a key role in the design and building of *Titanic* and it is possible to imagine that he has been photographed holding the plans of the great ship.

Thomas Andrews perished in the stricken *Titanic,* together with a team of eight shipyard workers. They formed Harland & Wolff's guarantee group and were on the maiden voyage to deal with any teething problems in the new ship. Andrews was held in high esteem at Queen's Island, where his leadership qualities and high moral standards were well respected. When he discovered the damage to *Titanic* was fatal, his response was characteristically selfless and it has ensured a place for him in the pantheon of *Titanic* heroes.

TR60-6A

'All his experience of ships, gained in the yards, on voyages, by long study, was in her; all his deep knowledge, too, gathered during twenty years and now applied in a crowning effort with an ardour that never flagged ... from the time of her conception slowly down through the long process of calculating, planning, designing, building, fitting, until at last she sailed away to the applause of half the world ... As Chief Designer and Naval Architect he planned her complete. As Managing Director he saw her grow up, frame by frame, plate by plate, day after day throughout more than two years ... As surely as none other did, he knew her inside and out, her every turn and art, the power and beauty of her, from keel to truck knew her to the last rivet. And because he knew the great ship so well, as a father knows a child born to him, therefore to lose her was heart-break.' Shan F. Bullock, *Thomas Andrews, Shipbuilder*, 1912

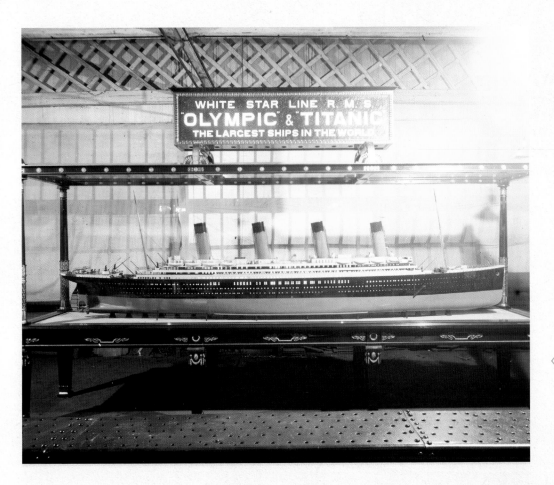

< Detailed model of the sister ships *Olympic* and *Titanic*, built in Harland & Wolff's model shop for promotional display by the White Star Line. (H2402)

< *Olympic* and *Titanic* were designed to be the largest ships in the world. On this White Star promotional postcard, the huge size of Olympic is illustrated by comparing the ship with famous tall buildings worldwide. (OMAFP-2010-27-361)

Pages 78-83 Harland & Wolff's general arrangement drawings of *Titanic*, showing the interior of the ship deck by deck. Titanic was built as Harland & Wolff's Ship No. 401.

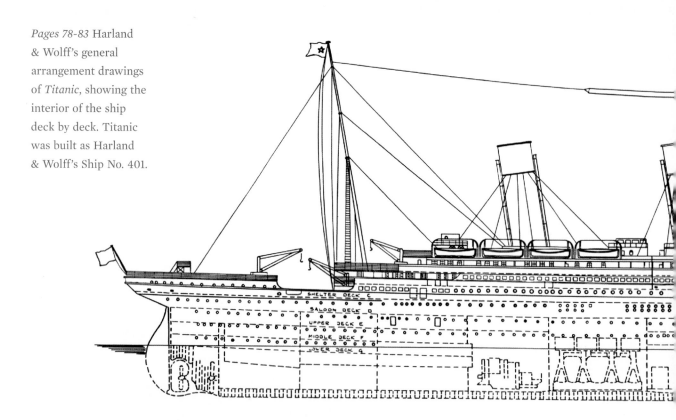

DIMENSIONS AND PARTICULARS OF TITANIC	
Length overall	882ft 9in
Breadth of hull	92ft 6in
Depth of hull	73ft 6in
Height from bottom of keel to boat deck	97ft 4in
Height from bottom of keel to top of Captain's house	105ft 7in
Height from bottom of keel to top of mast	236ft 0in
Height of funnels above casing	72ft 0in
Height of funnels of boat deck	81ft 6in
Distance from top of funnel to keel	175ft 0in
Number of decks	10
Number of watertight bulkheads	15
Load draft	34ft 7in
Gross tonnage	46,328 tons
Displacement	52,310 tons
Registered horsepower of engines	50,000
Number of boilers	29
Number of propellers	3
Designed service speed	21 knots
Actual speed achieved	22 knots +
Passenger and crew capacity	c. 3,000
Passengers and crew on board on maiden voyage	2,201
Number of lifeboats	2 0
Lifeboat capacity	1,178

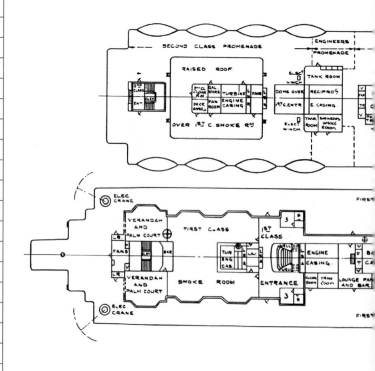

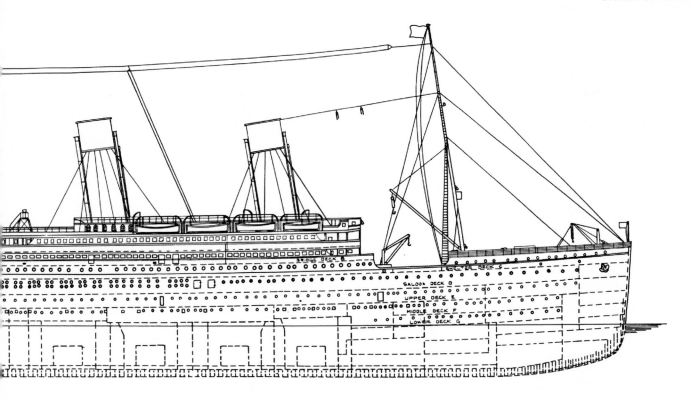

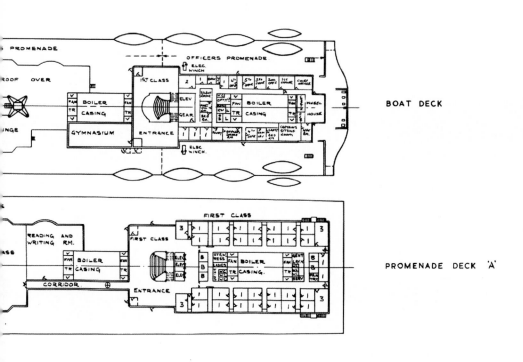

BOAT DECK

PROMENADE DECK 'A'

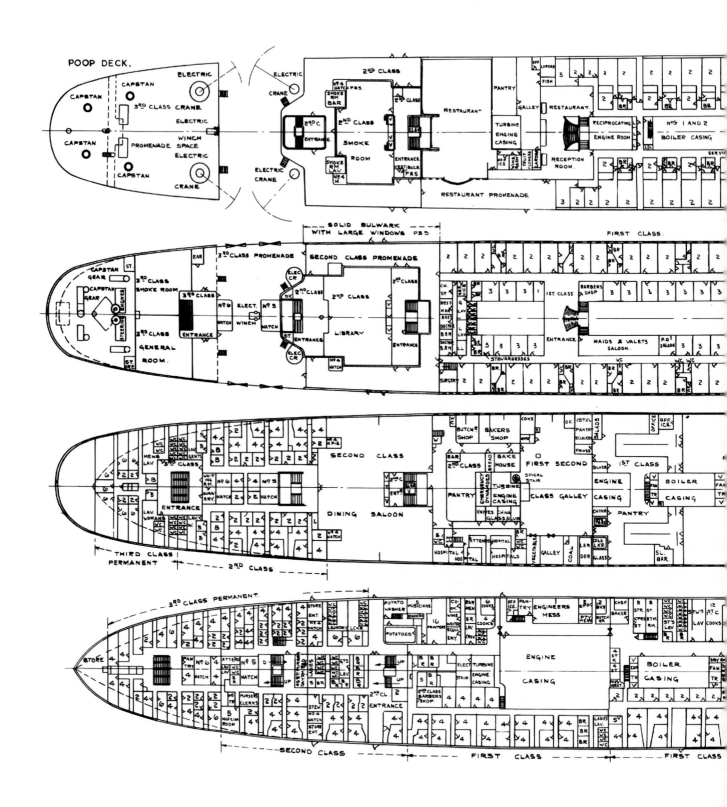

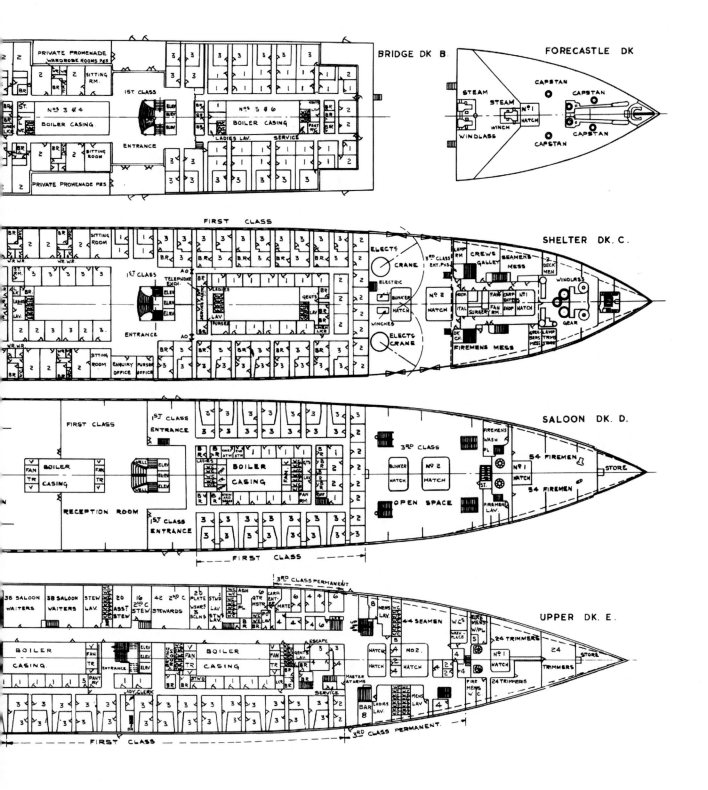

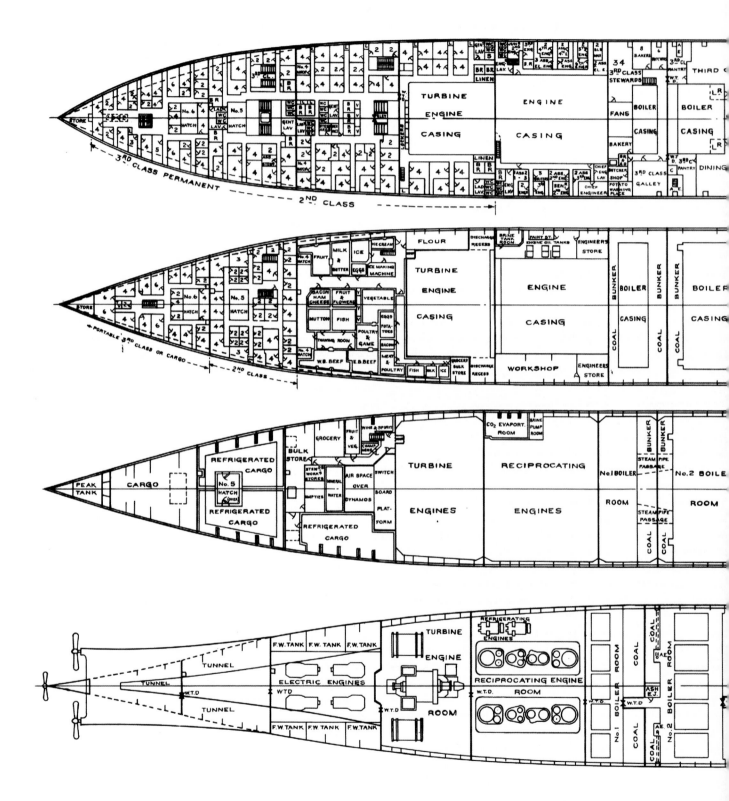

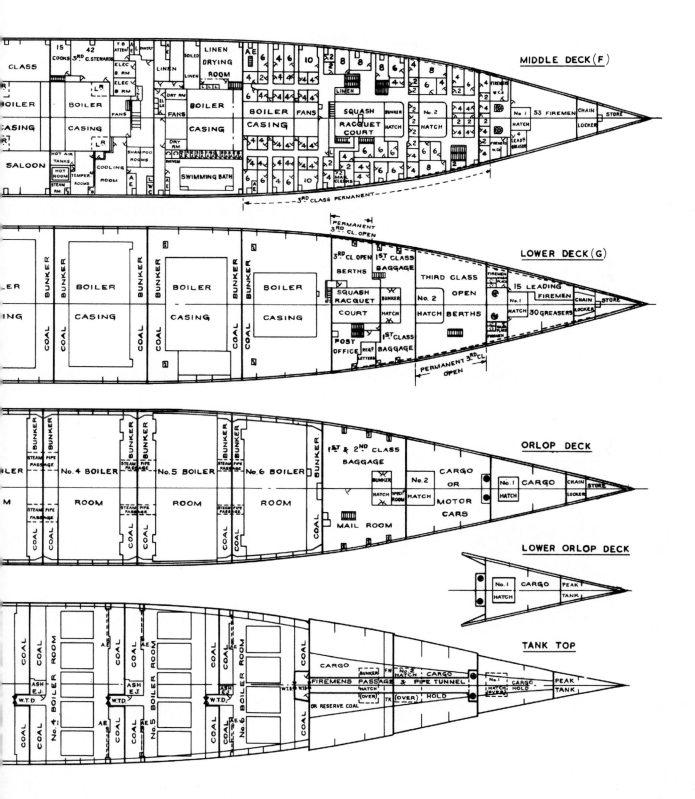

MIDDLE DECK (F)

LOWER DECK (G)

ORLOP DECK

LOWER ORLOP DECK

TANK TOP

THE
YARD
PREPARES

I**N** 1907 plans for the construction of the new White Star leviathans were discussed by Ismay and Pirrie and enthusiastically endorsed by Pierpoint Morgan. Shortly afterwards preparations began at Belfast for building *Olympic*, *Titanic* and a third sister, provisionally called *Gigantic*, but later changed to *Britannic* after the *Titanic* disaster.

An extensive reorganisation of the Queen's Island shipyard and investment in new plant were necessary. Two huge slips numbered 2 and 3 were laid out, replacing three existing slips. The ground in way of the new slips was piled throughout and covered with concrete up to 4½ feet deep. To facilitate the economical erection and hydraulic riveting of the ships, an enormous overhead gantry was built above the slips and equipped with a system of cranes, besides four large electric lifts. In addition to modifications to the joiners' shop and others, the platers' shed was remodelled and equipped with the machinery necessary to prepare the steelwork of *Olympic* and *Titanic*. A 200-ton floating crane was purchased from Germany to lift engines, boilers and funnels on board the ships when berthed at the new outfitting wharf after their launch.

Preparations were not confined to Harland & Wolff, for it was necessary that adequate berthing and drydocking facilities would be available for the new ships on their completion. Continuing their policy of harmonious co-operation with Harland & Wolff, Belfast Harbour Commissioners had begun the construction of a new drydock in 1903. Designed to be the largest in the world, it was completed in 1911 in time to permit the drydocking of *Olympic* on 1 April. At Southampton, harbour preparations and improvements included dredging, enlargement of the Trafalgar drydock and the construction of a new sixteen-acre wet dock or basin. In America IMM prevailed upon the New York Harbour Board to extend the White Star berthing piers by 100 feet. Such was the influence of Pierpoint Morgan that the work was carried out at the city's expense, despite many taxpayers' objections.

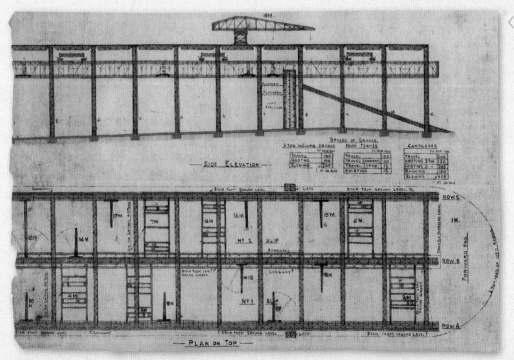

Elevation and plan of the Arrol gantry, erected over Slips 2 and 3 for the building of *Olympic* and *Titanic*.

'Preparations for construction and launching ... were undertaken upon a costly and magnificent scale. They involved the laying out of two berths large enough for vessels of such length and weight, and the erection of a gantry which is undoubtedly the largest in the world. Thus there has been added to Belfast's gigantic achievements a structure massive and towering, almost time-defying in its strength and one of the sights which arrest the engrossed attention of the traveller who visits the city for the first time.' *Belfast News-Letter* 21 October 1910

The enormous steel gantry being erected, in 1908, over the new building berths for *Olympic* and *Titanic* was supplied by Sir William Arroll & Co. of Glasgow at a cost of £100,000. Its purpose was to carry the cranes and lifts necessary for constructing the huge hulls of the new vessels. When completed, the weight of the entire structure and its equipment was almost 6,000 tons, with a height of 228 feet to the top of the upper crane. (H2547)

Two huge new slipways were required for the building of *Olympic* and *Titanic*. They were laid out as Slip Nos 2 and 3 in the North Yard, replacing three previous slips. This photograph, taken in 1907 in the early stages of construction, shows not only the filthy working conditions but also the dependency of an advanced industrial complex on hard physical labour and simple equipment. Here tradition and modernity are encompassed in a single image. (H1227)

'The trench in front of the Victoria Wharf, along the line of the launch, had to be dredged to a depth of fifty feet at high water spring tides, and Messrs Harland & Wolff undertook to strengthen the structure of the wharf which was originally only designed for a depth of fourteen or fifteen feet below ordinary water level ...' *Belfast News-Letter*, 21 October 1910

> 'There is something fitting in the selection of names for the latest marvels built at the Queen's Island, suggesting as they do the superiority and proportions of the two ships as compared with anything previously built. Notwithstanding the efforts of foreign rivals, this country still carries off the palm for speed and tonnage. Of course record-breaking is not looked for in the case of the new White Star boats, but they will nevertheless eat up nautical miles at a speed positively astonishing, when one considers the resistance of their vast hulls, and the tremendously large cargoes they are able to accommodate.' *Belfast News-Letter,* 21 October 1910

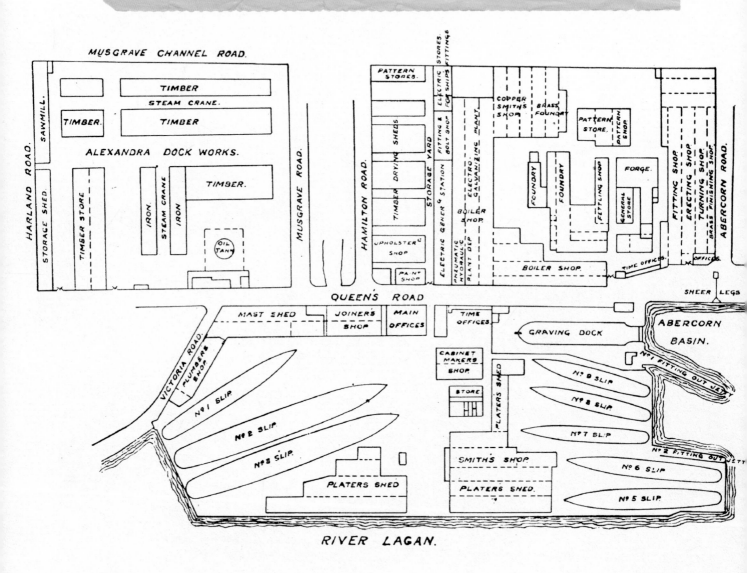

∧ Lay-out of Harland & Wolff's shipyard, Queen's Island, Belfast, 1911. Olympic and Titanic were built on Slip Nos 2 and 3, adjacent to the platers' shed (bottom left of the plan)

Harland & Wolff's Southampton Works (bottom ⟩ drawing) was acquired in 1907, following White Star's decision to move the home port for its New York mail service liners from Liverpool to Southampton. Improved repair facilities were powered by electricity and cost about £40,000 to install.

HARLAND & WOLFF, LIMITED.

Builders of the "OLYMPIC" and "TITANIC," the largest steamers in the World, 45,000 tons each.

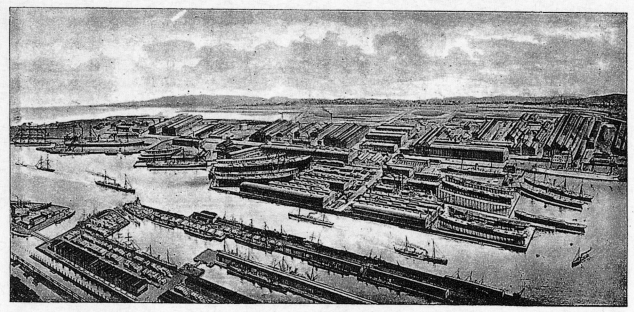

BELFAST WORKS.

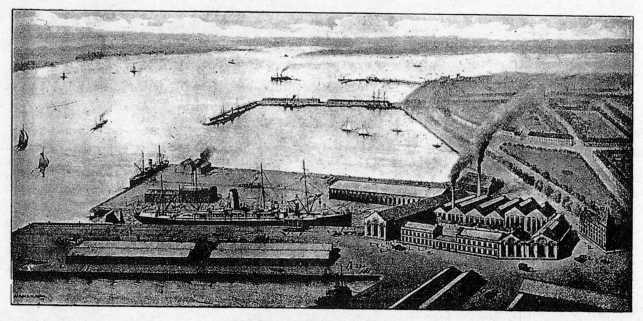

SOUTHAMPTON WORKS.

Harland & Wolff, Ltd., have headed the returns for Shipbuilding twelve times in the last twenty years. They have often exceeded 80,000 and 90,000 tons in the year, and thrice their output has been over 100,000, viz.:—

1903	8 vessels	110,463 tons,	100,400 I.H.P.
1908	8 „	106,528 „	65,840 „
1910	8 „	115,861 „	100,130 „

'The unique position occupied by Messrs Harland & Wolff in the shipbuilding world is due to many causes, but if we were asked to name that which in our opinion was the most potent we should not hesitate to declare for the personal element. Personality has undoubtedly been responsible for the high reputation which the firm possesses ... not only has it the services of an able and experienced staff, but at the head of affairs is Lord Pirrie, a wonderful personality whose influence pervades the establishment from end to end.

Under his guiding hand the business has steadily grown to its present pre-eminent position as the premier shipbuilding and engineering establishment in the world. On a site without natural advantages, where all the fuel and material required have to be imported, he has raised up a colossal concern which gives employment to between 14,000 and 15,000 men, and pays out in wages over £25,000 a week ... The *Olympic* successfully completed her trials the same day that the *Titanic* was launched (May 31 last), and no man, even at the zenith of his career, could hope for greater distinction than Lord Pirrie, the designer and builder of these magnificent vessels, has gained by their production ... In conclusion it would be difficult to name a firm that has done more for the development of commerce than Messrs Harland & Wolff ... the firm have, by their work, exercised a potent influence upon the strengthening process which is knitting the units of the British Empire more closely together, and by this same forging of new commercial links they have done much to bring into a closer band of union the great Anglo-Saxon race.' *Syren & Shipping*, 28 June 1911

FIRST SAILING OF THE LATEST ADDITION TO THE WHITE STAR FLEET

The Queen of the Ocean

TITANIC

LENGTH 882 FT. OVER 45,000 TONS TRIPLE-SCREWS BEAM 92½ FT.

This, the Latest, Largest and Finest Steamer Afloat, will sail from
WHITE STAR LINE, PIER 59 (North River), NEW YORK

Saturday, April 20th At 12 Noon

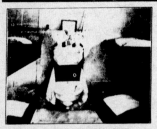

THIRD CLASS FOUR BERTH ROOM
Spacious Dining Saloons
Smoking Room
Ladies' Reading Room
Covered Promenade

All passengers berthed in closed rooms containing 2, 4, or 6 berths, a large number equipped with washstands, etc.

THIRD CLASS DINING SALOON

Reservations of Berths may be made direct with this Office or through any of our accredited Agents

THIRD CLASS RATES ARE:

To PLYMOUTH. SOUTHAMPTON, LONDON, LIVERPOOL and GLASGOW,	$36.25
To GOTHENBURG, MALMÖ, CHRISTIANIA, COPENHAGEN, ESBJERG, Etc.	41.50
To STOCKHOLM, ÅBO, HANGÖ, HELSINGFORS,	44.50
To HAMBURG, BREMEN, ANTWERP, AMSTERDAM, ROTTERDAM, HAVRE, CHERBOURG	45.00

TURIN, $48. NAPLES, $52.50. PIRAEUS, $55. BEYROUTH, $61., Etc., Etc.

DO NOT DELAY Secure your tickets through the local Agents or direct from
WHITE STAR LINE, 9 Broadway, New York

TICKETS FOR SALE HERE

WHITE STAR LINE.

— Royal and United States Mail Steamers. —

LARGEST STEAMERS IN THE WORLD:
"OLYMPIC," 45,000 Tons, and "TITANIC," 45,000 Tons (Building).

Triple-Screw Steamer **"OLYMPIC,"** 45,000 Tons,

THE LARGEST VESSEL IN THE WORLD.
WILL SAIL FROM

SOUTHAMPTON and CHERBOURG (*via* QUEENSTOWN) to NEW YORK

On Wednesday, June 14th, 1911.

Returning from New York on Wednesday, June 28th, 1911,

AND REGULARLY THEREAFTER.

ROYAL AND UNITED STATES MAIL SERVICE.

SOUTHAMPTON—CHERBOURG—QUEENSTOWN—NEW YORK,
via Queenstown, Westbound, and Plymouth, Eastbound, Wednesdays.

REGULAR SERVICES FROM

LIVERPOOL TO { NEW YORK, BOSTON, QUEBEC, MONTREAL, HALIFAX, PORTLAND,
CAPE TOWN, AND AUSTRALIA.
LONDON TO CAPE TOWN AND NEW ZEALAND.
NEW YORK AND BOSTON TO MEDITERRANEAN.

ISMAY, IMRIE & CO., 1, Cockspur Street, S.W., and 38, Leadenhall Street, E.C.,
London ; and 30, James Street, Liverpool.

The Services and Connections of the White Star Line encircle the Globe.

The voyage that never happened: an advertisement for *Titanic*'s return trip from New York.

Advertisement for the maiden voyage of *Olympic* on 14 June 1911. White Star's North Atlantic service was inaugurated in 1871. From the beginning, the company's ships were built in Belfast by Harland & Wolff. They were noted for innovative design and construction, with high standards of accommodation in all three classes.

'It is a matter of real gratification to all of us in Belfast that the *Olympic* and the *Titanic* should be built here, and in undertaking the construction of vessels of such enormous proportions, it is felt that Messrs Harland & Wolff are maintaining their own splendid traditions and at the same time indicating the right of the Ulster capital to be reckoned as one of the greatest shipbuilding centres in the world.' *Belfast News-Letter*, 21 October 1910

⌄ In order to lift heavy equipment and machinery on board *Olympic* and *Titanic* when docked at the new fitting-out berth, a giant 200-ton floating crane was ordered from the Benrather Company in Germany at a cost of £30,000. Because of its great height, the complex steelwork of the revolving jib was erected in Belfast. In this photograph, taken in 1908, construction is nearly complete and men can be seen working at the peak of the jib over 150 feet in the air. (H2492)

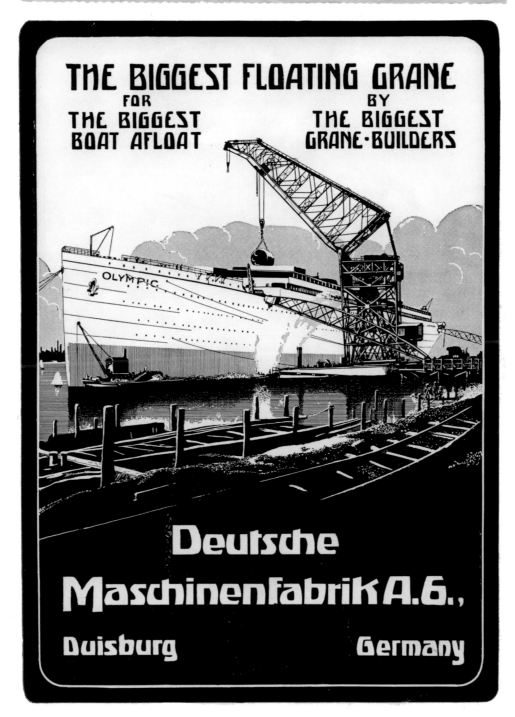

⌃ Advertisement for Harland & Wolff's German-built floating crane, showing a boiler being lifted on board *Olympic* when fitting out, after her launch on 20 October 1910. (OMAFP-2010-27-351)

∧ Platers' shed in the North Yard, 1912.
It had been reorganised and equipped
with new machinery to prepare the
steelwork of *Olympic* and *Titanic*.
Note the crane for lifting heavy
sections of steel. (H56)

Fitters' shop, 1899. Note the ships'
wheels on the left of the photograph.
Harland & Wolff were continuously
upgrading their workshop facilities:
in June 1911 the *Syren & Shipping*
reported that 'machinery is constantly
being renewed – good tools giving
place to still better ones – a process
which, habitually carried out,
naturally makes for the highest
efficiency'. (H556)

'The World's Biggest Graving Dock – Belfast has now the honour of having built the largest ship ever launched, and it will soon also have the distinction of being in possession of the biggest graving dock ever constructed. The work in connection with this necessary adjunct to modern and successful shipbuilding enterprise is now in its final stages and it is expected that the dock will be ready for the admission of vessels in December, or in January at the very latest, but the formal opening will not take place until the spring or summer.' *Belfast News-Letter*, 21 October 1910

Twin engineering achievements in Belfast. *Olympic*, the largest ship in the world, in the world's largest drydock, April 1911. (H1515)

'The new wharf has been constructed with the view of affording facilities for large vessels lying alongside prior to entering the new graving dock for repairs or painting, It is 600 feet in length and has been so designed as to permit of a depth of about 32 feet being obtained at ordinary low water in front of the wharf.' *Belfast News-Letter*, 21 October 1910

The largest graving – or dry – dock in the world viewed from the deck of *Olympic*, with *Titanic* on her slipway in the background, May 1911. With admirable foresight about the increasing size of ships, the Belfast Harbour Commissioners had decided to build the dock in 1903. It was finally completed in time for the drydocking of *Olympic* on 1 April 1911. Subsequently named the Thompson Graving Dock after the chairman of the Harbour Commissioners, it was 850 feet long, but capable of a further extension of $37\frac{1}{2}$ feet by shifting the caisson, or dock gate, to the outer groin of the dock, as shown in the photograph. The total construction cost was about £350,000. (H1656)

BUILDING
THE HULL

BEFORE modern systems of shipbuilding, the hull of a steel steamship was built as a skeletal structure, with the keel as a backbone, the frames acting as ribs to give shape and rigidity and the shell plating forming the watertight skin. The entire structure, from keel to bridge, was held together by heated steel pins known as rivets. About three million rivets – worked both by machine and by hand – were used in the building of *Titanic*. Before the advent of welding, hand-riveting was the defining trade of steel shipbuilding. Ceaseless hammering by teams of hand-riveters, together with the rattle of heavy machinery and the clanging of steel, made the shipyard a very noisy workplace. Often it was necessary to shout above the noise and hearing problems were common. The shipyard was also a dangerous place to work, with injuries and death resulting from falls, collapsing staging and machinery accidents, together with dropped rivets, tools and other materials.

Keel laying was the first practical stage in *Titanic*'s construction. From this point, the operations of building the hull, launching it, fitting it out with passenger accommodation and machinery and finally making the completed ship ready for sea, formed a complex building process involving thousands of people and several years of work. Essentially the design and construction of a great liner demanded the requirements of a floating hotel to be contained in a high-powered, navigable steel hull, built to withstand the enormous stresses and strains imposed by the motion of the waves and the turbulence of storms at sea.

In 1912 Shan Bullock, biographer of Thomas Andrews, wrote of the responsibilities faced by Harland & Wolff in their shipbuilding enterprise:

> Good enough in the shipyard is never enough. Think what scamped work, a flawed shaft, a badly laid plate, an error in calculation, may mean some wild night out in the Atlantic; and when next you are in Belfast go to Queen's Island and see there, in the shops, on the slips, how everyone is striving, or being made to strive, on your behalf and that of all who voyage, for the absolute best – everything to a hair's breadth, all as strong and sound as hands can achieve.

As Ship No. 400, *Olympic*'s keel was laid on 16 December 1908 on the newly-built Slip No. 2 in the North Yard. Three months later, on 31 March 1909, the keel of *Titanic*, Ship No. 401, was laid on the adjoining Slip No. 3. Construction of the two enormous hulls went on side by side. Both ships were designed to similar dimensions, but the Belfast press reported that on completion *Titanic*, with an overall length of 882ft 9in, was 3 inches longer than *Olympic*. The third sister ship *Britannic* (Ship No. 433), was laid down on 30 November 1911 on the slip used for the building of *Olympic*. With a breadth of 93ft 6in, she was designed to be 12 inches wider in the beam than her predecessors, but without a proportionate increase in hull length.

In a lecture given to the Belfast Natural History and Philosophical Society on 5 November 1915, Mr Alec Wilson, a practical shipbuilder, described the process of hull construction at Queen's Island:

> The keel is laid upon the top of the keel blocks placed to receive it ... Upon this keel is erected the keel plate, which forms a sort of spinal column for the future vesel [sic]. The lower part, or tank, is then proceeded with and after its completion ... the rib framing begun ... When the framing approaches completion the deckbeams are begun ... the whole ship is of course one immense steel girder, and its strength depends largely on the design and construction of the sub-girders.
>
> When the framing is completed the plating is begun, and the hydraulic riveters are concentrated upon those portions where there are special stresses, principally along the bilges and sheer strakes. The plates are commonly doubled at these parts, the thickness of the steel skin thus being about 2¼ inches and the diameter of the rivets 1⅛ inch ... the plates used for the sheer strake, the upper part of the skin of the ship, run up to about 36ft long, 6ft 6ins broad, by 1⅛ thick, and weigh over 4 tons ...

The chronology of building the hulls of the three White Star leviathans was documented in the notebook of a shipyard manager.

SHIP	KEEL LAID	BOTTOMS UP	FRAMED	PLATED	LAUNCH
Olympic	16 December 1908	10 March 1909	20 November 1909	15 April 1910	20 October 1910
Titanic	31 March 1909	15 May 1909	6 April 1910	19 October 1910	31 May 1911
Britannic	30 November 1911	12 March 1912	27 February 1913	10 September 1913	26 February 1914

From these dates it can be seen that building the hull of *Titanic*, from keel laying to launch, took 26 months. Work on the lead ship *Olympic* was four months less at 22 months, while hull construction of *Britannic* took longest at 27 months.

> ‘The *Titanic*, which is still unfinished, is almost a replica of the *Olympic*, the difference in length, for instance, being only three inches. The *Titanic* was completed side by side with the *Olympic* under the great gantry which is such a feature of the North Yard, and the spectacle of these two enormous ships on adjoining slips was altogether unprecedented and naturally the public interest taken in the vessels has been very keen.' *Belfast Evening Telegraph*, 26 December 1911

Hydraulic riveting of *Olympic*'s vertical keel plate, or centre keelson, 18 February 1909. Together with the flat keel plate and keel bar below – laid on 16 December 1908 – it forms the spinal column of the ship. The structure rests on wooden keel blocks carefully aligned at the correct inclination for a smooth launch in the future. The riveters are standing beside a portable furnace. (H1329)

The next stage of construction was the ship's bottom. Here work on *Olympic*'s after-end tank floors, or double bottom, is beginning in late February 1909. By 10 March the double bottom was all bolted up, and the work of riveting by hydraulic power well advanced. (H2364)

> ❝ *Olympic*... The double bottom, extending the whole length of the ship 5ft 3in deep – increased under the reciprocating engine room to 6ft 3in – the massive beams and close framing, the large shell plates, steel decks and watertight bulkheads, combine to make a structure of exceptional strength and rigidity.' *Belfast News-Letter*, 21 October 1910

∧ This photograph, taken on 8 May 1909, shows *Olympic*'s double bottom and progress in plating the tank top. This view is from the forward part of the ship, looking aft. Significantly it is the first photograph which depicts *Titanic* under construction on Slip No. 3 in the background. Work on *Titanic*'s vertical keel plate has been completed, following the laying of the keel on 31 March 1909. (H1330)

> ❝ The double bottom is utilised for carrying water ballast, the floor plates between the intercostal girders having lightening holes, except at intervals, where they are without holes, to form separate ballast-tanks.' White Star publicity, 1911

∧ *Olympic* (left) and *Titanic* (right) side by side on Slip Nos 2 and 3 in the early stages of construction, 8 May 1909. Through the complex web of gantry steelwork, it can be seen that work is just beginning on *Titanic*'s after-end tank floors. This view complements the photograph opposite as it was taken on the same day, but from the after end of the ships looking forward. (H1331)

⟨ View of *Olympic* from seaward end of Slip No. 2, showing her double bottom and work on plating the tank top, May 1909. The jib of the 200-ton floating crane can be seen in the background. (H2389)

⋀ Plating *Olympic* tank top with erected after-end frames visible in the background, 30 July 1909. Timber shores are supporting the bottom of the ship's hull. On Slip No. 3 beyond *Olympic*, *Titanic*'s double bottom can be seen. (H1332A)

No 400-20

Lower part of *Olympic*'s stern frame fitted in position, with the upper part of the frame being lifted on to the slip, August 1909. The stern frame was made of Siemens-Martin mild cast steel by the Darlington Forge Company. With a combined weight of 70 tons, these heavy steel sections presented a difficult and hazardous handling task for the shipyard workers. (H2393)

After-end frames of *Olympic* and erected stern frame, August 1909. The upper and lower sections of the stern frame were connected by 112 rivets 2 inches in diameter, the total weight of rivets being over a ton. (H2396)

Nº 400-23

The steel hulls of *Titanic* and *Olympic* taking shape on adjacent slipways are easily identified by their proudly displayed notices. When this photograph was taken in mid-April 1910, *Titanic* was fully framed and the shell plating of *Olympic* had been completed. The ships' frames were spaced three feet apart, except at the bow and stern where they were respectively 24 inches and 27 inches apart. (H2377)

> Some idea of the great importance of the riveting in the *Olympic* and *Titanic* will be gathered from the fact that there are half a million rivets in the double bottom of each vessel, weighing about 270 tons, the largest rivet being 1¼ inches in diameter ...' *Shipbuilder*, 1911

∧ This is a rare shipyard photograph of hand-riveting, with hand-riveters hard at work on the shell plating of *Titanic*'s sister ship *Britannic* on 25 May 1913. The noise of hammering would be so great that the workers could not hear each other speak. Riveters worked in gangs of three men and a boy. Two of the men are on the outside of the hull, each with a heavy hammer. Inside the hull is the third man, called the 'holder-up', who has a still heavier hammer to hold each rivet in position. The boy is also inside the hull and his job is to heat the rivets in a portable furnace until they are red-hot. The boy then takes a rivet from the furnace with a pair of pincers and pushes it through a hole in the frame and the plate, where it is hammered hard by the men on the outside to secure it tightly. They strike alternately, first one and then the other, swinging their hammers so fast that the noise of the blows is continuous. (H1915)

By 5 August 1910, when this slightly unsharp photograph was taken, shell plating of *Titanic*'s hull was well advanced, and *Olympic*'s long since completed. Heavy timber shores support the hulls, while the complex arrangement of wooden staging allows riveters and others to work on the outer shells of the huge vessels. (H2382)

Simultaneously with framing and shell plating, work was proceeding on the interior structure of the ships. In this rare photograph of *Titanic*'s internal construction, *c*.October 1910, men are working on the steel beams and hatchways of the upper decks. The scale and complexity of *Titanic*'s steel framework are set against the humanity of the workers who are building the ship. Her hull is enveloped by the lattice steelwork of the great gantry. (H2423)

' *Olympic* ... The hydraulic riveting in the vessel is also an important factor, the whole of the shell plating up to the turn of the bilge being riveted by hydraulic power, and an immense amount of work of the same kind has been carried out in other parts of the ship, including shell, topsides, decks and stringers. These rivets were closed by means of the powerful 7-ton machines suspended from the travelling frames on the gantry ... it may be mentioned that there are over half a million rivets in the double bottom alone, these weighing 270 tons, the largest rivets being 1¼ inches in diameter; and in the complete ship there are something like three millions, weighing about 1,200 tons.' ' *Belfast News-Letter*, 21 October 1910

The entire steel structure of *Titanic* and her sister ships was riveted together. Much of it was done by hand, but where possible hydraulic riveting machinery was used. In this photograph, taken 25 May 1913, the upper shell plating of *Britannic* is being hydraulically riveted by a machine suspended from the gantry. The large number of rivets needed to join plates and frames together can be clearly seen. (H1919)

Shell plating of *Titanic* was completed on 19 October 1910, one day before the launch of *Olympic*. This photograph of the two sister ships side by side was taken earlier in the month as *Olympic* was being prepared for launching. Her hull was painted light grey to aid photography of the event. (H1479)

❛ *Olympic* ... If the comparatively tiny pieces of molten metal [rivets] holding together the great framework are so numerous and so heavy, what about the acres of plates that go to make up the leviathan? The largest shell plates are 36 feet long, weighing 41 tons each, and the largest beam 92 feet long, the weight of the double beam being four tons; the stern frame weighs 70 tons; the after boss arms 73½ tons, the forward 45 tons, the rudder 100 tons.' *Belfast News-Letter*, 21 October 1910

∧ The dark steel hull of *Titanic* contrasts
with the light grey paintwork of *Olympic*
as preparations for her launch are
advanced during mid-October 1910. The
towering presence of the two leviathans
dwarfs the horse-drawn cart and the men
working below. (H1440)

❛ The watertight subdivision of the *Olympic*
and *Titanic* is very complete, and is so
arranged that any two compartments may
be flooded without in any way involving the
safety of the ship ...' *Shipbuilder*, 1911

Olympic was launched on 20 October 1910 in the presence of the Lord Lieutenant of Ireland and other distinguished guests. There was great public interest in the event, with particular reporting of the technical arrangements for launching the largest ship in the world. So successful were these arrangements that they were repeated for *Titanic* the following year. (WAG 3192)

> ❝ *Titanic* ... The shell plating is extremely heavy. It is, for the most part, of plates 6ft wide and of about 30ft in length. The laps are treble-riveted, and the sheer strakes have been hydraulically riveted. This also applies to the turn of the bilge, where bilge keels 25in deep are fitted for 295ft of the length of the vessel amidships.' *Belfast News-Letter*, 1 January 1912

⌃ By mid-May 1911 construction of *Titanic*'s hull was almost complete. This remarkable photograph of men fitting the starboard tailshaft demonstrates the huge size of *Titanic* and clearly shows the rudder design and arrangement of riveted shell plating around the stern frame. The rudder was constructed by the Darlington Forge Company and comprised five sections bolted together, giving a total weight of 101¼ tons. However, the most powerful aspect of the photograph is the way it contrasts the inert mass of *Titanic*'s steel hull with the vulnerability and humanity of the workers constructing her. In this carefully choreographed group of men, there is a spectral figure of a worker – beside the man on the right – who has been deleted by the photographer on his glass plate negative in order to improve the composition. This 'ghost' can be read as symbolising the mortality of all who built and sailed in *Titanic*. (H1557)

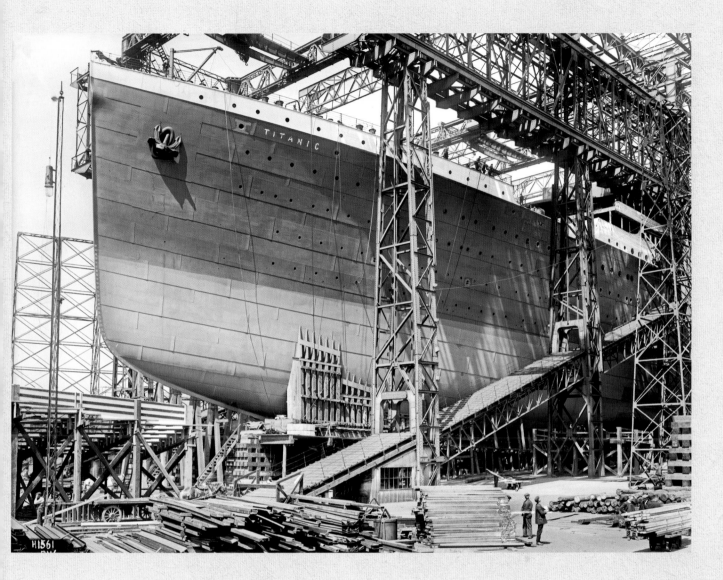

∧ In this splendid photograph preparations are almost complete for the launch of *Titanic* on 31 May 1911. Beneath her bows a grandstand for spectators has been erected and horses stand patiently in the shafts of their carts. High on the deck a shipyard worker looks down on the scene of quiet activity below the great ship which he has helped to build. The play of sunlight and shadow emphasises the steel plating of *Titanic*'s hull, painted in readiness for her launch. The ship will soon be released from the enfolding steelwork of the Arrol gantry, with its distinctive access ramps. As she slides down the ways, enormous pressure will be taken by the timber cradle which supports *Titanic*'s bows. The painted name *Titanic* has been enhanced by the photographer on his glass plate negative. (H1561)

8

LAUNCH
DAY

TITANIC was launched on 31 May 1911. The event was timed to coincide with the sea trials of *Olympic* and her departure from Belfast. Pierpoint Morgan, Bruce Ismay and other distinguished guests, together with members of the international press, travelled to Belfast in the specially chartered cross-channel steamer *Duke of Argyll*.

Because of *Titanic*'s great size, very careful arrangements were made for her launch, following the system used for the launch of *Olympic* seven months previously. There was no ceremonial breaking of a bottle on the ship's bow, but rather the signal to launch was given by Lord Pirrie and the firing of rockets. Mr Charles Payne was in charge of the hydraulic apparatus which started *Titanic*'s motion down the greased ways into the water. Shortly after noon on a warm sunny day, huge crowds of cheering shipyard workers and spectators witnessed the launch. It took 62 seconds for *Titanic*'s hull – over 882 feet long and weighing 24,360 tons – to slide from her building berth into the water of Belfast harbour.

∨ The unusual presence of women in the shipyard, the grandstand and the readiness of the ship all suggest that this photograph was taken a day or so prior to the launch of *Titanic* on 31 May 1911. (H23641)

⟨ Workman's ticket for
the launch of *Titanic*. It
was issued to Mr David
Moneypenny, a shipyard
painter who worked
on *Titanic*'s first-class
accommodation.
(TR59-4)

Following the launch, the distinguished guests were entertained to luncheon by Lord Pirrie at Queen's Island. Less important guests and members of the press, together with some of the principal officials of Harland & Wolff, were served luncheon at the Grand Central Hotel in Belfast's Royal Avenue. At 4.30 in the afternoon, Ismay, Morgan, Pirrie and guests sailed for Liverpool on board the completed *Olympic*, now ready for service on the North Atlantic.

Launches are always dramatic events in the life of a shipyard, but the launch of *Titanic* evoked particular feelings of pride, achievement and hope in the hearts of the Belfastmen who were building her as the largest ship in the world. As with all ship launches, this was a symbolic rite of passage – a sort of birthgiving as well as a practical operation for moving the ship's hull from the land to the water. Feelings of relief were tinged with poignancy as, within seconds, *Titanic* changed from an inert structure of riveted steel to a vessel floating in her natural element for the first time.

Within an hour of *Titanic*'s launch, the crowds had disappeared and her hull towed to the deepwater wharf for the second phase of construction – the fitting-out of passenger accommodation and the installation of all necessary equipment and machinery, including engines, boilers and funnels.

> ❜ THE LAUNCH OF THE TITANIC
> To prevent any disappointment to the public desirous of witnessing the launch of this vessel tomorrow, it may be stated that the hour fixed for the ceremony is 12.15 p.m.; that a red flag will be hoisted at the stern of the vessel ten minutes before the time; that a rocket will be fired five minutes before the release of the vessel, and a second, one minute before the releasing valve is opened, when the ship should commence to move down the ways. Ticket-holders should note that positions on the stand in Messrs Harland & Wolff's yard cannot be secured after the firing of the first signal, and after the second signal rocket has been fired the doors will be closed, and no one will be admitted to the works.' *Belfast News-Letter*, 30 May 1911

Hydraulic launching rams were positioned at the head of the slipway, directly beneath the bows of *Titanic*. (H1566)

'During the morning gangs of men were engaged in removing the heavy wooden posts which supported the vessel, a powerful ram being also used in the operation. The clanging of hammers was heard all over the ship as the preparations for the launch were developed, but the men using them were for the most part hidden from view. On the deck of the boat the figures of the workers whose duty it was to see to the drag ropes and cables were dwarfed and blurred by the distance which separated them from the people down below.

About twelve o'clock Lord Pirrie left the owners' stand in order to make a last tour of inspection and to give final instructions and responsible officials watched the movements of the hands on the hydraulic triggers as the supports were removed and the ship settled down on the launching ways. Every detail had to be judged with mathematical accuracy if accidents had to be averted, and the preparations had therefore to be made with great care and caution.

Over the bows of the vessel the White Star Company's flag floated, and there was displayed a code signal which spelled the words "success". If the circumstances under which the launch took place can be accepted as an augury of the future, the *Titanic* should be a huge success ...'
Belfast News-Letter, 1 June 1911

Lord Pirrie, chairman of Harland & Wolff and Bruce Ismay, chairman and managing director of White Star, made a tour of inspection immediately before the launch of *Titanic*. For headwear, Pirrie favoured a casual yachting cap while Ismay preferred the more formal bowler hat. The apparatus on the left is a pressure gauge for the hydraulic launching triggers which held *Titanic* on the ways when the timber shores and blocks were removed. (#23640)

It is close to midday on 31 May 1911 and shortly *Titanic* will make the mighty and unrepeatable transition from land to sea. The coffer dam has been removed and the high tide, flooding the lower part of her slipway, is ready to receive *Titanic*. On the adjacent Slip No. 2 the coffer dam remains in place, while seepage water cascades from the pumps positioned behind the dam. *Titanic*, like *Olympic*, will be launched without her propellers as they will be fitted later in the drydock. (H1568)

‘ARRANGEMENTS FOR TODAY'S CEREMONY ... We understand that the arrangements made for the admission and comfort of the sightseers at the Albert Quay enclosure are excellent ... the harbour authorities have kindly allowed this enclosure to be made by the authorities of the local children's hospitals, who are charging a small sum for admission. Many thousands of people can be accommodated and obtain the finest view of the launch. Mr Nance has arranged for an ample tram service from Castle Junction, via Corporation Street, to Pilot Street, which is about five minutes walk from the enclosure, and the Harbour Board are providing a two minutes' ferry service from Abercorn Basin steps for the convenience of those coming from the County Down side, and from Milewater Basin steps to the enclosure steps, where admission may be gained at the ordinary price.’
Belfast News-Letter, 31 May 1911

'The owners' stand ... in addition to Mr Pierpoint Morgan, the occupants included Lord and Lady Pirrie, Mr Ismay, Mr E.C. Greenfell, Miss Ismay, Miss E. Ismay, Miss Edmonson, Master George Ismay, Miss Correns, Mr Sanderson, Mr Charles F. Torrey, Mr Graves, Mr Hale, Mr Curry, Commander Holland, Mr George Medly, Mr Fletcher and Mr H. Concannon.' *Belfast News-Letter*, 1 June 1911

∨ *Titanic* launched, 31 May 1911. Her great hull, 882ft 9in long and weighing 24,360 tons, reached a launch speed of 12½ knots. To enable *Titanic* to slide smoothly down the ways vast quantities of lubricants were used – 15 tons of tallow, 5 tons of tallow and train oil mixed, together with 3 tons of soft soap. (H1559)

⌄ The weather was gloriously fine as *Titanic*
slipped away from her building berth into
her natural element in just 62 seconds. The
owners' stand, erected not at the bows of
Titanic but on her port side, was draped
in white and crimson, the flag colours of
the White Star Line. Here Lord and Lady
Pirrie were congratulated by Pierpoint
Morgan and other distinguished guests, not
only for their launch of *Titanic*, but also
on the happy coincidence of Lady Pirrie's
birthday. (H1558)

'LAUNCH OF THE TITANIC. IMPRESSIVE SPECTACLE AT THE QUEEN'S ISLAND. A SUCCESSFUL CEREMONY. BRILLIANT WEATHER AND ENTHUSIASTIC SCENES.

In the presence of thousands of spectators, the SS *Titanic*, which will share with the *Olympic* the distinction of being one of the largest vessels afloat, was launched from Messrs Harland & Wolff's yard at the Queen's Island yesterday ... The builders had left nothing to chance, and the launch was one of the most successful ever witnessed at the Island ... No one doubted for a single moment that the huge vessel would take the water without any trouble occurring in regard to her departure from the slips, but they could hardly have anticipated that the scene presented would be so inspiriting and impressive as it actually was. It was the significance of the thing which struck their imagination and caused many of them to become very eager and excited as the time approached for releasing the hydraulic apparatus which would set the vessel in motion and send her gliding down the ways into the river ...

The design and dimensions of the *Titanic* and the *Olympic* are practically identical ... The vessels mark a new epoch in naval architecture. In size, construction and equipment they represent the last word in this science ... It may be mentioned that there are fifteen transverse water-tight bulkheads, extending from the double bottom to the upper deck at the forward end of the ship, and to the saloon at the after end – in both instances far above the load water line ... So thorough are the precautions which have been taken to prevent the ship from sinking in the event of a serious accident that any two compartments may be flooded without endangering the safety of the vessel ...' *Belfast News-Letter,* 1 June 1911

∨ *Titanic* afloat in Belfast for
the first time, 31 May 1911.
Without her engines, boilers,
funnels, machinery and fittings,
she's riding high in the water.
Around her enormous hull men
in rowing boats are beginning
to recover pieces of launch
debris. Heavy anchors, chains
and cables arrested the launch
momentum of *Titanic* as she
was pulled up in less than
half her own length. Within
an hour, tugs had removed
her to the fitting-out wharf
for completion, the task made
easier by recent dredging and
deepening of the channel.
(H1569)

'Without any flourish of trumpets, beyond the
enthusiastic cheering of an immense concourse
of people, the *Titanic,* sister ship of the *Olympic,*
was successfully launched from the Queen's Island
yesterday morning, and Belfast enjoyed for one
day the world's record of having over 90,000 tons
of shipping in her port made up by two ships. The
greatest shipbuilding centres of the world have
never come within measurable distance of this feat
of local industry; and Ireland generally, and our city
especially, have every reason to be proud of this most
convincing of proof of Irish brains and Irish industry.
That Ireland can beat the world in the second decade
of the Twentieth Century is perhaps a sign of the
times, which cannot be taken too seriously by her
sons. All over the world the hearts of our countrymen
will be gladdened at the news of yet another signal of
victory of the old country.' *Irish News*, 1 June 1911

'Mr Pierpoint Morgan, the American millionaire, was one of the spectators at the launch. Mr Morgan occupied a place on the owners' stand, which had been erected under one of the huge gantries on the port side of the *Titanic*. This stand was draped in white and crimson ... Three other stands had been erected at the end of the yard opposite the bows of the vessel. One of these was reserved for the representatives of the Press, who numbered upwards of one hundred, whilst the others were for the accommodation of ticket-holders. The stands were by no means adequate for all who had assembled, and hundreds of people took up positions in various parts of the yard from which they could see the ship enter the water. The Lord Mayor and the Lady Mayoress (Mr & Mrs McMordie) were amongst the onlookers, and many other prominent citizens helped to swell the attendance ...

The ceremony had been fixed for a quarter-past twelve and ten minutes before that time a red flag was hoisted at the stern of the vessel. Five minutes later two rockets were discharged, shortly afterwards the explosion of another rocket was heard and at 12.13 the spectators had the joy and satisfaction of seeing the vessel in motion. It was a wonderful and awe-inspiring sight, and a thrill passed through the crowd as their hopes and expectations were realised. The ship glided down to the river with a grace and dignity which for the moment gave the impression that she was conscious of her own strength and beauty, and there was a roar of cheers as the timbers by which she had been supported yielded to the pressure put upon them. She took the water as though she were eager for the baptism, and in the short space of 62 seconds she was entirely free of the ways.

The arrangements for checking her once she had entered the river were similar to those adopted in the case of the *Olympic*. On each side of the ship anchors had been placed in the bed of the river, and to them were attached hawsers which were fastened to eye plates on board. Cable drags, connected with the vessel in a similar fashion, were also used, and by means of them and the anchors the *Titanic* was pulled up in less than one-half of her own length.

The men on board took off their caps and cheered lustily after the launch had been consummated, and the thousands of people in the yard and on the banks of the river promptly followed their example. For two or three minutes there were scenes of great enthusiasm. The tugs which were waiting close at hand to convey the vessel to the deep-water wharf, where she will receive her engines, sent up shrill sounds from their sirens, the ladies waved their handkerchiefs excitedly, and the men shouted themselves hoarse.

But gradually the noise of the sirens and the cheers of the spectators died away, and a quarter of an hour after the vessel had been pulled up the crowd had melted away, and the yard was left in possession of the workmen who had for months been devoting their energies and talents to the building of the mighty leviathan.' *Belfast News-Letter*, 1 June 1911

BEHIND THE SCENES

IN 1911 Harland & Wolff launched ten vessels, including *Titanic*, with an aggregate tonnage of 118,209 and a total horsepower of 97,000. These figures gave Queen's Island the distinction of the largest output on record in one year from any shipyard in the world.

It was a boom period. By the end of the 1910/11 financial year, Harland & Wolff's profits totalled almost £110,000, while the number of men at work in the yard had risen sharply from 11,389 in 1910 to almost 15,000 at the end of 1911. The wages bill at this latter date was £25,000 weekly, which was considered to be an enormous and unprecedented figure. The shipyard's output and production would have been impossible without a well-organised workforce, together with efficient shipyard plant and facilities.

A strong order book in the financial year 1910–11 encouraged Pirrie to invest in a number of improvement schemes at Queen's Island. These took two years to complete and cost almost £250,000. They included the replacement of the old offices by a new three-storey building, an extension to the boiler shop, a new smiths' shop, new cranes and strengthened berths.

Reporting on a visit to Queen's Island – 'The Birthplace Of The Big Ship' – in June 1911, the *Syren & Shipping* declared:

> There is, moreover, every reason to anticipate that the firm's output of tonnage during the current year will beat all records. It need scarcely be remarked that an establishment with a production capacity such as is indicated ... can be no ordinary collection of ships, sheds and engine and boiler shops. It is, on the contrary, one of the best laid out and most perfectly equipped yards in the world ... No visitor going over the establishment can fail to be impressed with the well ordered activity which prevails everywhere ... the spirit of modernity or of a mature youthfulness suffuses everything.

Titanic's propelling machinery was a combination arrangement of two reciprocating steam engines and a low-pressure steam turbine. Here, in May 1911, her port-side reciprocating engine is nearing completion in the Engine Works erecting shop. The massive size of the machinery is indicated by the workman standing alongside. The engine bedplate weighs 195 tons, the columns 21 tons each and the heaviest of the four cylinders 50 tons. Soon the engine will be dismantled and the components taken to the fitting-out wharf for re-erection in *Titanic*'s engine room. (H1711)

The scale and factory organisation of industrial shipbuilding at Queen's Island is reflected in this photograph of the Engine Works turning shop in 1912. (H1805)

This view of the new foundry in 1912 depicts both working conditions and the vastness of the shipyard infrastructure that contributed to Harland & Wolff's position as the largest shipbuilding firm in the world. (H58)

∧ Turbine machinery and castings in the Engine
Works erecting shop, 1912. Turbines were the
latest and most technically advanced form of
steam propulsion. Harland & Wolff developed
this new type of marine engine in the form of
a low-pressure turbine working in combination
with conventional reciprocating engines. This
combination arrangement was pioneered in
the White Star liner *Laurentic* of 1909 and
subsequently installed in the sister ships
Olympic, *Titanic* and *Britannic*. (H1658A)

⌃ *Titanic* and her sister ships were fitted with three propellers. The centre or turbine propeller, made of manganese bronze, was the smallest, although it had four blades with a diameter of 16ft 6in. The two wing propellers, driven by the reciprocating engines, were three-bladed, but had a larger diameter of 23ft 6in. This is a photograph of *Olympic*'s centre propeller *c.*November 1910. (H1457)

∧ Propeller shafting intended
for *Britannic* being turned on
a lathe in the Engine Works,
19 August 1913. Identical
shafting, with a diameter of
26¼ inches, had previously
been fitted in *Titanic* and
Olympic. (H1925)

In this photograph *Britannic*'s ⟩
turbine machinery is being
assembled in the Engine Works
in May 1914. Construction of the
turbine rotor, with its thousands
of steel blades, was a demanding
engineering task. It followed the
design of *Titanic*'s rotor, which
had a length of 13ft 8in between
the first and last ring of blades, a
diameter of 12 feet and a weight
of about 130 tons. (H2155)

Titanic and her sister ships were each fitted with twenty-four double-ended and five single-ended coal-fired boilers. These completed boilers, ready for installation in *Olympic*, were photographed in the Engine Works boiler shop about November 1910. The heavily riveted boiler shell plates were of mild steel $1^{11}/_{16}$ inches thick. (H1455)

Completed crankshafts for *Britannic*'s reciprocating engines. Photographed in the Engine Works on 25 May 1913, they illustrate the massive scale of marine engineering required to power *Britannic* and her earlier sister ships *Titanic* and *Olympic*. (H1922)

'Then into shop after shop in endless succession, each needing a day's journey to traverse, each wonderfully clean and ordered, and all full of wonders. Boilers as tall as houses, shafts a boy's height in diameter, enormous propellers ... turbine motors on which workmen clambered as upon a cliff, huge lathes, pneumatic hammers, and quiet slow-moving machines that dealt with cold steel, shearing it, punching it, planing it, as if it had been so much dinner cheese. Then up into the Moulding Loft, large enough for a football ground, and its floor a beautiful maze of frame lines; on through the Joiners' shops, with their tools that can do everything but speak; through the Smiths' shops, with their long rows of helmet-capped hearths, and on into the great airy building ... where an army of Cabinetmakers are fashioning all kinds of ship's furniture. Then across into the Central power station, daily generating enough electricity to light Belfast. On through the fine arched Drawing Hall where the spirit of Tom Andrews seemed still to linger, and into his office where often he sat drafting those reports, so exhaustively minute, so methodical and neatly penned, which now have such pathetic and revealing interest.' Shan Bullock, *Thomas Andrews, Shipbuilder*, 1912

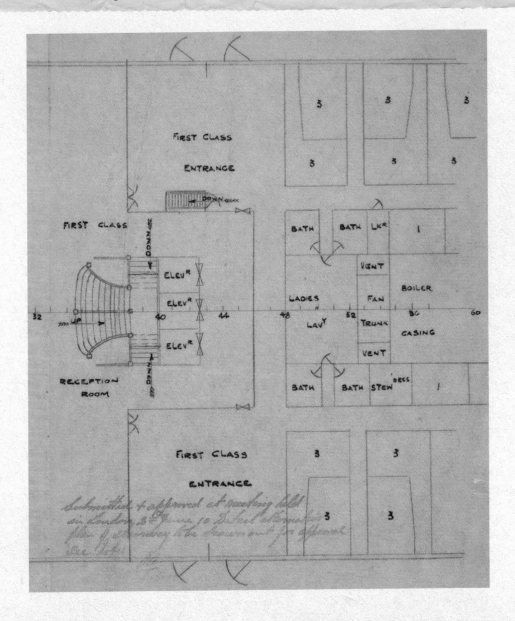

Drawing of first-class
entrances, staircase and
elevators, annotated and
initialled by Thomas
Andrews, 6 June 1910.
(TR 62-9)

Side view of *Titanic*'s two main reciprocating steam
engines nearing completion in the Engine Works
erecting shop, May 1911. Here they are arranged
in line, but when installed in the ship they sat
side by side. The engines were four-cylinder
triple expansion type designed to operate at a
steam pressure of 215lbs per square inch, with
each engine indicating about 15,000 horsepower
at 75 r.p.m. In *Titanic*'s combination arrangement
of propelling machinery, exhaust steam from
the reciprocating engines was further expanded
through the low-pressure turbine, thereby giving
increased power without an increase in coal
consumption. (H1710)

10

FITTING OUT

AFTER her launch on 31 May 1911, *Titanic* was immediately towed to the deepwater wharf for completion. Her fitting out lasted ten months, with between 3,000 and 4,000 men working on board the ship and in the workshops. On 10 November 1911 the *Northern Whig* noted that 'while two or three thousand operatives are working at the skeleton afloat, almost as many more skilled hands are engaged in the workshops ashore providing the muscles and flesh wherewith it is to be clothed'. Machinery, engines, boilers, funnels, shipboard equipment, furnishings and all the things necessary for putting a great liner to sea were brought to the deepwater wharf for installation in *Titanic*. Particularly heavy machinery and engineering materials were lifted on board by the 200-ton floating crane. Much of the ship's equipment and fittings was made in the shipyard workshops, but a vast range of items, particularly with regard to the accommodation and navigation of *Titanic*, were provided by sub-contractors and specialist suppliers.

During *Titanic*'s outfitting, *Olympic* returned to Belfast twice for repairs, each visit requiring the moving of *Titanic* to facilitate the drydocking and undocking of *Olympic*. The first occasion was on 4 October 1911, when *Titanic* was temporarily removed from the deepwater wharf to the nearby Alexandra wharf, in order to allow *Olympic* to enter the drydock for extensive repairs, following her collision with HMS *Hawke*. A week later, on 11 October, the fitting out of *Titanic* was sufficiently advanced for it to be officially announced that she would leave Southampton on her first voyage to New York on 10 April 1912.

One final but important stage in the completion of *Titanic* was her drydocking on Saturday 3 February 1912. This was necessary for the fitting of her three huge propellers and the painting of the hull. *Titanic* was floated into the dock under the superintendence of Lord Pirrie himself. A month later *Titanic*, now back at the outfitting wharf, temporarily returned to the drydock to accommodate the departure of *Olympic*, which had been brought back to Belfast for repairs to a propeller and slight damage to the shafting. In a skilful operation on 6 March the positions of the two leviathans were changed on one tide.

Unfortunately, however, the building and outfitting of *Titanic* were not achieved without shipyard injuries and fatalities. On 17 June 1911 the *Belfast News-Letter* reported on an inquest into the death of Robert James Murphy, aged 49, of 6 Hillman Street, a rivet counter who was fatally injured on board the *Titanic*.

George Maginess, a boy, gave evidence:

> Witness saw the deceased put up his hand to count the rivets, and just with that the staging went down, and deceased fell too. The ends of the deck gave way and fell to the staging below, the deceased dropping a distance of about 50 feet. The coroner said a fact that made the inquest a singularly pathetic one was that the deceased's son had been killed about six months ago on the same ship.

To maintain the momentum of public interest in *Titanic* as she was building, White Star and Harland & Wolff promoted descriptive details not only of the ship's passenger accommodation but also of its innovative technical arrangements, particularly with regard to the safety of the vessel. However, the number of lifeboats fitted, while in accordance with Board of Trade regulations, was insufficient for the number of passengers and crew to be carried.

> ' The navigating appliances are most complete, and the lifeboats are mounted on special davits, while there is a complete installation for receiving submarine signals. Each watertight door can be released by means of a powerful electric magnet controlled from the captain's bridge, so that, in the event of accident, the movement of a switch instantly closes each door, practically making the vessel unsinkable.' *Belfast News-Letter*, 1 January 1912

∧ '*Titanic* Fitting Out', watercolour by Charles Dixon, 1912. This atmospheric night-time painting depicts busy round-the-clock working as *Titanic* nears completion. (TR57-08)

∧ This photograph of *Titanic* fitting out at the deepwater wharf was taken early in 1912. Even without her fourth funnel erected, *Titanic* dominates the bleak industrial landscape, although the floating crane eclipses her in height. Two gangways connect the ship to the shore, while the workers' 'heads' or lavatories are fitted clear of *Titanic*'s starboard bow. (MS503)

> ' There are fifteen transverse watertight bulkheads, extending from the double bottom to the upper deck at the forward end of the ship and to the saloon deck at the after end – in both instances far above the waterline ... The watertight doors in a vessel of this size are, of course, a most important item ... They are of Harland & Wolff's special design, of massive construction, and provided with oil cataracts governing the closing speed.' White Star publicity, 1911

∧ Unusual view of the shipyard with *Titanic* in
the background, fitting out at the deepwater
wharf. Another liner can be seen fitting out in
the middle foreground. The photograph was
taken from the top of the Arrol gantry, late in
February 1912. (MS462)

Fitting-out activity on board *Olympic*, looking towards the stern of the ship, 2 January 1911. The photograph illustrates the operation of the floating crane, which is positioned between *Olympic* and the fitting-out wharf. Its two hooks could lift a total of 200 tons to a height of 149 feet. (H2406)

∧ Watertight bulkhead door in raised open position during
fitting out of *Olympic*, *c.*December 1910. These doors
allowed communication between the various boiler rooms
and engine rooms. They were so designed that in the
event of an accident the captain could, as the *Shipbuilder*
reported, 'by simply moving an electric switch, instantly
close the doors throughout and make the vessel practically
unsinkable'. (H1471)

∧ Double-ended boiler, with its
corrugated furnaces, about to
be lifted on board *Britannic* at
the deepwater fitting-out wharf,
21 March 1914. (H1967)

> ❝ *Britannic* ... WHITE STAR LINE'S LATEST ORDER FOR
> BELFAST – 2000 TONS HEAVIER THAN THE *TITANIC* ...
> the White Star Line have ordered from Messrs Harland & Wolff,
> of Belfast, a vessel which will be the largest British-built ship in
> the world. The great liner is to measure 882ft 6in overall, with a
> beam of 93ft 6in, and a gross tonnage of 47,000. She will thus be a
> foot broader and 2,000 tons heavier than the *Olympic* and *Titanic*
> ... During the next two and a half years a small army of men will be
> engaged in building and fitting out the great liner, which will cost
> about £1,500,000. One third of this sum will be spent on wages.'
> *Belfast News-Letter*, 1 January 1912

In this striking photograph the last funnel of *Olympic* is being manoeuvred out of the workshops on 23 March 1911. However, as in *Titanic* and *Britannic*, No. 4 funnel was a dummy, although it replicated the other three funnels in size and external appearance. Each funnel had an elliptical cross-section which measured 24ft 6in by 19ft 0in. When fitted on board, the funnel height soared 70 feet above the casing (H2412)

⟨ *Olympic*'s No. 3 funnel about to be shipped on board by the 200-ton floating crane at the fitting-out wharf, 2 February 1911. (H2407)

⌃ In the immensity of *Britannic*'s engine room, shipyard workers are at an early stage of installing one of the ship's main reciprocating engines, 29 April 1914. (H1996)

❝ A ladder or escape is provided in each boiler room, engine room and similar watertight compartment, in order that the closing of the doors at any time shall not imprison the men working therein; though the risk of this eventuality is lessened by electric bells placed in the vicinity of each door, which ring prior to their closing, and thus give warning to those below.'
White Star publicity, 1911

⌃ Wooden lifeboats under construction in Harland and Wolff's boatbuilders' shed in 1899. Their standard design was double-ended and clinker-built. All ships carried lifeboats of varying size and capacity. Each of *Titanic*'s large lifeboats was built to carry 65 persons. (H512)

∧ View forward along the starboard boat deck of *Olympic* during outfitting, April 1911. Although the number of lifeboats carried by *Olympic* and *Titanic* were in excess of Board of Trade regulations, they were insufficient for the number of passengers and crew on board. (H1508)

❝ Only two of the *Titanic*'s four funnels are at present in position, but the wonderful skeleton on her five upper decks is nearly complete – a skeleton that represents the bare walls of what four months hence will be a floating town of five or six thousand inhabitants, replete with every appointment that modern luxury and refined taste could suggest in connection with a "West End" community on shore.'
Northern Whig, 10 November 1911

'ACCIDENT AT THE *TITANIC*. The services of the new motor ambulance were requisitioned for the first time yesterday afternoon, when it received a call to the White Star liner *Titanic*, which was lying in the new graving dock. It appears that a young man of 22 years of age, named George Stewart, residing at 95 Mountcollyer Road, was working on a crane when he was crushed in the machinery. The ambulance immediately conveyed the unfortunate man to the *Royal Victoria Hospital*, where it was found that he was suffering from severe internal injuries. The time taken by the new motor from headquarters to the hospital was under a quarter of an hour. Inquiries made at an early hour this morning elicited the information that the patient was progressing favourably.' *Belfast News-Letter*, 8 March 1912

A scene of heroic endeavour. Here men are striving to secure the upper casing of the low-pressure turbine on board *Britannic*, 4 August 1914. (H2164)

'It is safe to predict that this noble ship will enjoy the popularity earned by the *Olympic*, and still further enhance the reputation of both owners and builders. She is being rapidly completed and is expected to take her place in the sailing list early this year.'
Belfast News-Letter, 1 January 1912

This rather tranquil view of *Titanic* nearing completion at the fitting-out wharf in late January 1912 belies the frenzy of activity taking place within the ship to meet the delivery deadline: on 11 October 1911 the sailing date of her maiden voyage had been officially announced as 10 April 1912. Although all four of *Titanic*'s funnels are up they are not yet painted. (H1712)

∧ *Olympic*'s 15½-ton central
anchor on a seven-horse wagon
photographed outside the Queen's
Road offices on its way to the
fitting-out wharf, October 1911.
Transportation of the anchors
was sub-contracted to the well-
known Belfast haulage firm of
John Harkness & Co. (H1449)

'For generating electric current for light and power, four 400-kilowatt engines and dynamos are fitted in a separate watertight compartment aft of the turbine room at tank top level ... In addition to the four main generating sets there are two 30-kilowatt engines and dynamos, placed in a recess off the turbine-room at saloon-deck level. Three sets can be supplied with steam from either of several boiler rooms, and will be available for emergency purposes ...

A complete system of electric lighting is, of course, provided, and electricity is also largely employed for heating, as well as for motive power, including no fewer than 75 motor-driven "Sirocco" fans from 55in to 20in in diameter, for ventilating all the passenger and crew spaces, as well as the engine and boiler rooms. All fan motors are provided with automatic and hand speed regulation.' White Star publicity, 1911

∧ Starboard main generating set installed in the electric engine room of *Olympic*, May 1911. (H1534)

H1524.
R.W.

∧ *Olympic* nearing completion at the deepwater fitting-out wharf, May 1911. This is a view aft from the port boat deck looking towards the poop deck at the stern. Like *Titanic*, the ship was equipped with a total of eight electric cargo cranes. (H1524)

‘ Many hundreds of visitors to Belfast during the last few weeks have taken a tram-car ride down to the end of the Queen's Road ... and there lay the *Titanic*, with her stupendous deck erections still in the rough and only a dozen or two of artisans flitting like ants about her decks ...’ *Northern Whig,* 10 November 1911

'... Then the dinner horn sounded, and down the gangways ... began to pour streams of hurrying workmen streams that seemed inexhaustible ... Watching these human streams, one got an idea of what the construction of the *Titanic* means in enterprise, sustained effort and money.'
Northern Whig, 10 November 1911

Shipyard workers disembarking from *Olympic* in the final weeks of fitting out at the deepwater wharf, in May 1911. The floating crane is positioned between the ship and the wharf. Between 3,000 and 4,000 men were engaged in the completion of *Olympic*, and later of *Titanic*, both on board the ships and in the workshops. (H1516)

∨ *Titanic* in the Thompson Graving Dock, where she was drydocked on 3 February 1912. The pumphouse and its smoking chimney can be seen in the background. Drydocking *Titanic* in the final stages of construction allowed the fitting of her three propellers and other work on the hull. Note the crow's nest on the mast, from where the lookouts first sighted the iceberg. (OMAFP-2010-27-167)

Letter from Charles Payne, Harland & Wolff, dated 21 July 1911, to Captain McIntyre, Belfast Harbour Master, complaining about the excessive speed of cross-channel steamers creating dangerous situations for *Titanic* and the men working on board her while fitting out at the deepwater wharf. He asks for steps to be taken to address the problem.

HARLAND & WOLFF, Ltᴅ
TELEGRAMS, HARLAND BELFAST.
TELEPHONE 906.
LONDON OFFICE
14 COCKSPUR STREET, S.W.
TELEGRAMS, HARLANDIC LONDON
TELEPHONE 6410 GERRARD.
BRANCH
SHIP REPAIRING & ENGINEERING WORKS,
SOUTHAMPTON.
TELEGRAMS, HARLAND SOUTHAMPTON.
TELEPHONE 590.

Shipbuilding & Engineering Works.

Belfast. 21st July, 1911.

ALL COMMUNICATIONS TO BE ADDRESSED TO THE COMPANY.

Captain McIntyre,
Harbour Master,
BELFAST.

Dear Sir,

No. 401 s.s. "Titanic".

No doubt it has been reported to you that one of the cross
channel steamers passed the above vessel about 12.15 p.m. yesterday, at a
high rate of speed, causing the "Titanic" to range heavily on her moorings,
and one of the 5" long fore and aft springs parted, causing the wire hawser
to fall suddenly on one of the scows on which several men were working,
which, of course, was most dangerous, as some of the men narrowly escaped
being killed and knocked into the water.

We may further say that recently we have observed that the
mid-day channel steamers frequently pass this vessel at too high a rate of
speed, which was especially the case when these Works were closed for
holidays last week.

We shall be glad if you will please take the necessary steps to
prevent a recurrence, and we shall be glad to have your assurance accordingly.

Yours truly,

For HARLAND & WOLFF LTD.

Notice by Captain J. McIntyre, Belfast Harbour Master, dated 22 July 1911, cautioning against excessive speed in the Harbour, especially in the vicinity of *Titanic*.

BELFAST HARBOUR COMMISSIONERS.

HARBOUR MASTER'S OFFICE,

BELFAST, *22nd July, 1911.*

EXCESSIVE SPEED OF STEAMERS IN THE HARBOUR.

Several complaints have been received lately in regard
to the excessive speed of steamers while in the Harbour more
especially in the vicinity of the "Titanic" at New Deep Water
Wharf.

The moorings of that steamer have been carried away twice,
and yesterday several men narrowly escaped being killed by a wire
mooring parting above where they were working.

Please be good enough to caution the masters of your vessels
to exercise every precaution, and go slow, while navigating in the
Harbour to prevent injury to life and property.

J. M'INTYRE,

Harbour Master.

'DRYDOCKING OF THE *TITANIC*. The White Star liner *Titanic*, a sister ship of the Olympic, built by Messrs Harland & Wolff, was moved into the new graving dock on Saturday morning. The operations, which occupied about a couple of hours, were witnessed by Lord Pirrie, who was at the scene as early nine o'clock. At that hour the ropes were loosened and three tugs – *Hercules*, *Jackal* and *Musgrave* – towed the gigantic vessel from the fitting-out wharf to the dock entrance. A comparative calm and a good tide, high water being at two minutes to 11 o'clock, favoured the work, which was superintended by Lord Pirrie himself ... Notwithstanding the vast dimensions of the liner she was safely docked without so much as scraping her sides on the walls. The "shoring up" operations were afterwards commenced and carried out with expedition. It then only remained to pump the drydock in order to proceed to completing the furnishing and finishing of the *Titanic*.' *Belfast News-Letter*, 5 February 1912

The original 1912 caption for this photograph identified the drydocked ship as *Titanic*, but in fact it is *Olympic* in the Thompson Graving Dock. However both liners underwent the same drydocking operation to fit the propellers and other necessary hull work. (L1118/4)

This photograph was taken in April 1911 when *Olympic* was drydocked to have her three propellers fitted. The massive size of the propellers, the rudder and the ship's hull is emphasised by the human figure standing alongside on the graving dock floor. (H1511)

'The mammoth White Star liner *Olympic* entered the new graving dock at high tide on Saturday morning ... after her mishap in mid-Atlantic where she lost a blade of her propeller and sustained some slight damage to the shafting ... *Olympic* reached the entrance to the dock shortly after nine o'clock. It was only a matter then of gliding in, and so successfully was this accomplished that there was not even the slightest scraping of the sides of the vessel against the walls ... Several photographers attended and took views of the vessel as she settled into position prior to the erection of the stays.' *Belfast News-Letter,* 4 March 1912

∨ At the beginning of March 1912, *Olympic* and *Titanic* were together for the last time, when *Olympic* (left) returned to Belfast for propeller repairs and *Titanic* (right) was nearing completion. This photograph was taken as *Olympic* entered the flooded drydock at high tide, shortly after 9 a.m. on Saturday 2 March 1912. (H1637)

> ❝ ... *Titanic* is now nearing completion at Belfast and will leave Southampton and Cherbourg on her first voyage to New York on Wednesday, 10th April.' *Belfast News-Letter*, 8 January 1912

∨ *Titanic* nearing completion at the deepwater fitting-out wharf in the second week of March 1912. The last-minute improvement of enclosing the forward part of Promenade Deck A with sliding windows still remains to be done. *Titanic* now faces seaward, after being towed from the drydock on 8 March, where she was temporarily accommodated to facilitate the manoeuvring of *Olympic* following her propeller repairs. (H1713)

11

ACCOMMODATION

TITANIC and her sister ships represented a huge capitalist enterprise, as well as a tremendous shipbuilding achievement. The whole purpose in building them was to generate profits for White Star in the lucrative and highly competitive North Atlantic passenger trade. The bigger and better the ships, the greater the profit potential.

Although *Titanic* was similar to *Olympic* in general design and construction, passenger modifications and improvements were made to the ship as a result of experience gained with *Olympic* and a keen sense of the market place. Essentially *Titanic*'s earning capacity was increased by changes and enhancements focused on the first-class accommodation. Besides increasing the number of staterooms, the more expensive parlour suite rooms on Bridge Deck B were extended out to the sides of the ship, where formerly there had been a promenade deck. However, the very wealthy passengers paying premium fares for these exclusive parlour suites had access to two private promenades decorated in a half-timbered Tudor style.

Further aft, on the starboard side of the same deck, former promenading space for second-class passengers was replaced by the novel shipboard feature of a Café Parisien for first-class passengers. This 'charming sun-lit verandah, tastefully decorated in French trellis-work with ivy and other creeping plants' was situated outside the first-class

∧ Second-class boat deck, White Star publicity, 1911 (H401-E)

First-class private promenade, 〉 *Titanic*, March 1912 (L3036/12)

restaurant, which itself was extended to incorporate a spacious reception room decorated in the Georgian style.

Here, as the *Shipbuilder* described,

> friends and parties will meet prior to taking their seats in the restaurant. The elegant settees and easy chairs are upholstered in silk of carmine colour, with embroideries applied in tasteful design. The breadth of treatment and the carefully proportioned panels on the walls, with richly carved cornice and surrounding mouldings, form an impressive *ensemble*, which is distinctly pleasing to the eye. There is accommodation for a band in this room.

Because of the increased number of first-class passengers that could be carried in *Titanic*, additional seating was provided in the main dining saloon, so that over 550 passengers could dine at the same time.

Externally, the modification to *Titanic* which distinguished her from *Olympic* was the partial enclosure of Promenade Deck A, in order to protect first-class passengers from the weather. This feature appears not to have been preplanned and was incorporated very late in *Titanic*'s outfitting in March 1912. It was not in place on 6 March when the *Belfast News-Letter* reported on *Titanic*'s 'interesting innovations':

> So popular has the Louis XVI Restaurant proved on her sister ship the *Olympic*, that in the case of *Titanic* this apartment has been enlarged and adjacent is a special reception-room for the use of passengers taking meals in the restaurant. The deck on one side is connected with it, so as to form a sort of balcony for those who prefer their meals in the open air. The *Titanic* also contains special suites of rooms, consisting of bedrooms, sitting room, bathroom and servants' room, and these will have their own private promenade, shut off from the rest of the ship, and not overlooked by other passengers.

White Star's marketing of *Olympic* and *Titanic* was masterful. The ships were promoted as 'without peer on the ocean … on a scale of unprecedented magnificence … nothing like them has ever appeared on the ocean'. The Line indulged in extravagant eulogies of the two ships as 'standing for the pre-eminence of the Anglo-Saxon race in command of the seas'. They were seen to contribute to 'the movement of the British and American people towards the ideal of international and universal peace'. Reflecting the self-confidence of the age, White Star proclaimed that *Olympic* and *Titanic* were 'eloquent testimonies to the progress of mankind' and would 'rank high in the achievements of the 20th century'. With unconscious irony, prospective passengers were assured of the 'comfort, elegance and security' offered by the new leviathans.

While the excellent accommodation for second and third class was also described, the publicity promotion was primarily directed at potential first-class passengers, especially wealthy and well-to-do Americans. *Olympic* and *Titanic* were projected as floating grand hotels, or great houses, decorated in various historical styles, but equipped with every modern convenience, from electric lifts to a telephone exchange.

On board, passengers would be so far removed from the rigours of sea travel that only on deck or through the windows would they be reminded that they were on a ship crossing the Atlantic ocean:

> We leave the deck and pass through one of the doors which admit us to the interior of the vessel, and as if by magic, we at once lose the feeling that we are on board ship, and seem instead to be entering the hall of some great house on shore …

Such delights were not for the third class of course. These passengers, paying an economy or emigrant fare, were far removed from the Turkish baths, swimming pools and squash racquet courts. Shying away from any suggestion of crowding, White Star declared that the third-class general room – panelled and framed in pine and finished enamel white with teak furniture – would 'doubtless prove one of the liveliest rooms in the ship'. Compared to ships of a few years previously and indeed compared to some of the emigrant ships of other lines, the quality of third-class accommodation on board *Titanic* was very good indeed. The shipboard conditions for third-class passengers were so improved that White Star confidently assured them that 'in these vessels the interval between the old life and the new is spent under the happiest possible conditions'.

∧ Café Parisien, *Titanic*, March 1912 (H1733)

FIRST CLASS

∨ First-class smoke room: 'Here, seated around the home-like fire, we may smoke and drink as wisely and well as we feel inclined.' White Star publicity, 1911

∨ In the middle of the hall rises a gracefully curving staircase, its balustrade supported by light scroll-work of iron with occasional touches of bronze, in the form of flowers and foliage. Above all a great dome of iron and glass throws a flood of light down the stairway, and on the landing beneath it a great carved panel gives its note of richness to the otherwise plain and massive construction of the wall. The panel contains a clock, on either side of which is a female figure, the whole symbolising Honour and Glory crowning Time. Looking over the balustrade, we see the stairs descending to many floors below, and on turning aside we find we may be spared the labour of mounting or descending by entering one of the smoothly-gliding elevators which bear us quickly to any other of the numerous floors of the ship we may wish to visit.

The staircase is one of the principal features of the ship, and will be greatly admired as being without doubt the finest piece of workmanship of its kind afloat.' White Star publicity, 1911

First-class lounge: 'When talk becomes monotonous, we may here indulge in bridge and whist, or retire with our book or our letters to one of the many quiet retreats which reveal themselves to the thoughtful explorer.' White Star publicity, 1911

First-class elevators, White Star publicity, 1911 (H401-D)

First-class reception room:
'It is here that the Saloon passengers will foregather for that important moment upon an ocean-going ship – *l'heure ou l'on dine* – to regale each other with their day's experiences in the racquet court, the gymnasium, the card room, or the Turkish bath ... Upon a dark, richly coloured carpet, which will further emphasise the delicacy and refinement of the panelling and act as a foil to the light dresses of the ladies, this company will assemble – the apotheosis, surely, of ocean-going luxury and comfort.'
White Star publicity, 1911

First-class dining saloon:
'This immense room has been decorated in a style peculiarly English – that, in fact, which was evolved by the eminent architects of early Jacobean times ... The furniture of oak is designed to harmonise with its surroundings and at the same time to avoid the austere disregard for comfort in which our forefathers evidently found no hindrance to the enjoyment of a meal.'
White Star publicity, 1911

First-class restaurant:
'On one side is ample
accommodation for
an orchestra, partly
recessed and raised
on a platform.'
White Star
publicity, 1911
(OMAFP-2010-27-340)

First-class verandah café
and palm court: 'Passing
through the silently-
revolving doors, we
emerge upon a gay little
verandah over whose
green trellis grow climbing
plants, which foster the
illusion that we are still
on the fair, firm earth;
but one glance through
the windows, with their
beautifully-chased bronze
framing, adds to the
charm, and we realize that
we are still surrounded
by the restless sea, once
so dreaded a barrier to
national intercourse. Set
in this flowery arbour
are numerous inviting
little tables, at which we
can take our coffee or
absinthe in the open air,
much as we do in our own
summery gardens on land.'
White Star publicity, 1911

First-class gymnasium, ❭
Titanic, March 1912. On
the fateful night of 14/
15 April 1912, the
physical educator,
Mr T.W. McCauley,
remained at his post
and went down with
the ship. (H1730)

⟨ First-class swimming bath, White Star publicity, 1911.
'Then the morning plunge in the great swimming bath,
where the ceaseless ripple of the tepid sea water was
almost the only indication that somewhere in the distance
72,000 horses in the guise of steam engines fretted and
strained under the skilful guidance of the engineers, and
after the plunge a half-hour in the gymnasium helped
to send one's blood coursing freely, and created a big
appetite for the morning meal.' Passenger's impressions,
Belfast Evening Telegraph, 15 April 1912

∨ First-class gymnasium. Here passengers could 'indulge
in the action of horseriding, cycling, boat-rowing,
etc., and obtain beneficial exercise, besides endless
amusement'. White Star publicity, 1911

First-class Turkish ›
baths cooling room:
'... in many respects one
of the most interesting
and striking rooms
on the ship. The port-
holes are concealed by
an elaborately-carved
Cairo curtain, through
which the light fitfully
reveals "something of
the grandeur of the
mysterious East".'
White Star
publicity, 1911

First-class squash ›
racquet court: 'The
court is situated on
the lower deck, and
extends two decks high
for a length of 30 feet.
A spectator gallery is
placed on the after
end of the court on
the middle deck level.'
White Star
publicity, 1911

First-class sitting room of parlour suite: 'The finish and decoration of the first-class staterooms are well in keeping with the excellence of the public rooms; the staterooms are also exceptionally large and beautifully furnished. Perhaps the most striking are the suite rooms, of which there is an unusually large number decorated in different styles and periods.'
White Star publicity, 1911

First-class stateroom: 'Each of the first class staterooms has a cot bed in brass, mahogany or oak, and in most of the suiterooms the cots are four feet wide. This is a distinct feature which will be greatly appreciated by passengers.'
White Star publicity, 1911

First-class parlour suite ›
bedroom in Georgian
style, White Star
publicity, 1911

First-class parlour suite ›
sitting room in Louis
XIV style, White Star
publicity, 1911

First-class parlour suite ›
bedroom in Adam's
style, White Star
publicity, 1911

∧ First-class parlour suite
B60, *Titanic*, March 1912
(H1726)

First-class parlour ⟩
suite B64, *Titanic*,
March 1912 (H1729)

⟨ First-class parlour
suite B59, *Titanic*,
March 1912 (H1725)

First-class bathroom, ⟩
White Star
publicity, 1911
(#401-C)

⟨ First-class parlour
suite B38, *Titanic*,
March 1912 (H1728)

First-class parlour suite
B57, *Titanic*, March 1912
(H1724)

'It is impossible to adequately describe the decorations in the passenger accommodation. The ship must be seen and inspected for these features to be fully appreciated. They are on a scale of unprecedented magnificence. Nothing like them has ever appeared before on the ocean ... The Staterooms in their situation, spaciousness and appointments, will be perfect havens of retreat where many pleasant hours are spent, and where the time given to slumber and rest will be free from noise or other disturbance ... Comfort, elegance, security – these are the qualities that appeal to passengers, and in the *Olympic* and *Titanic* they abound.' White Star publicity, 1911

SECOND CLASS

∨ Second-class two-berth stateroom, White Star Publicity, 1911

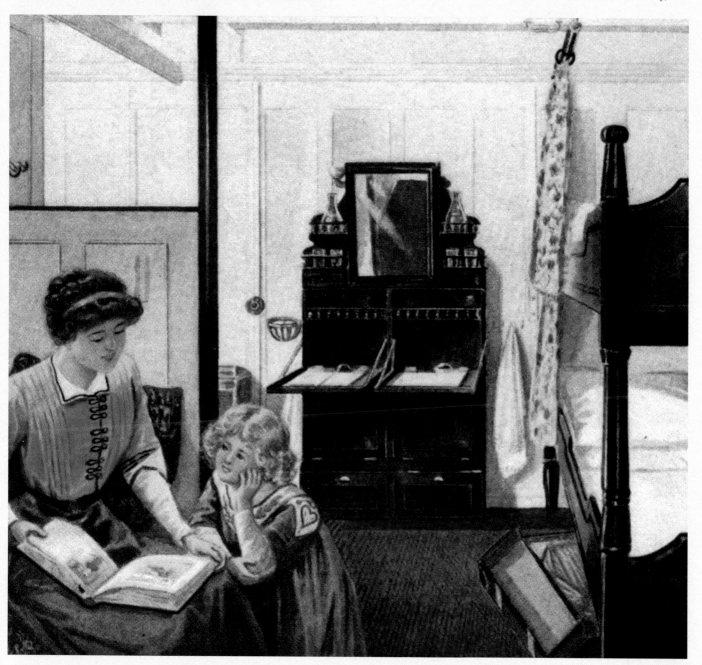

' The White Star Line has done much to increase the attractions of second-class accommodation during recent years, having made a special feature of this in a number of their vessels; and in the *Olympic* and *Titanic* it will be found that this class of passenger has been generously provided for. It would have been difficult a few years ago, to conceive such sumptuous appointments in the second class.

Second-class staterooms. The majority of these rooms are arranged on the well-known tandem principle, ensuring natural light to each cabin; the rooms are finished enamel white, and have mahogany furniture covered with moquette, and linoleum tiles on the floor.' White Star publicity, 1911

∧ Second-class single-berth stateroom,
White Star publicity, 1911 (#401 A)

Second-class smoke room: 'the decoration is a variation of Louis XVI period; the panelling and dado are of oak relieved with carving; the furniture is of oak of special design, covered with plain, dark green morocco.' White Star publicity, 1911

Second-class dining room. 'The panelling of this room is carried out in oak, the design of which is taken from examples in the early part of the 17th century, with details of a somewhat later period introduced ... At the forward end a specially-designed sideboard, with piano in the centre, is provided; the furniture is in mahogany, the upholstery of crimson leather and the floor has linoleum tiles of special design.' White Star publicity, 1911

THIRD CLASS

∨ Third-class general room. 'This is also aft on the shelter deck. It is panelled and framed in pine and finished enamel white, with furniture of teak. This, as its name implies, will be the general rendezvous of the third-class passengers – men, women and children – and will doubtless prove one of the liveliest rooms on the ship. The friendly intercourse, mutual helpfulness and bonhomie of third-class passengers is proverbial, and, remembering that many of them have arrived at the most eventful stage in their career, we realise that "touch of nature that makes the whole world kin". The new field of endeavour is looked forward to with hope and confidence, and in these vessels the interval between the old life and the new is spent under the happiest possible conditions.' White Star publicity, 1911

Third-class dining saloon: 'situated amidships on the middle deck, consisting of two saloons extending from ship's side to ship's side, well lighted with sidelights, and all finished enamel white; the chairs are of special design ... Third-class passengers today have greater comfort on the ocean than first-class passengers had before the great developments had taken place for which the White Star Line is largely responsible.' White Star publicity, 1911

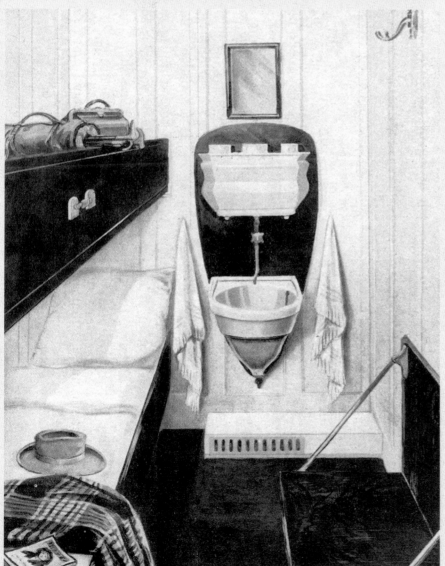

Third-class stateroom. 'They are mostly arranged for two and four passengers; but in some rooms six, eight or ten people can be accommodated. The provision of such a large number of two-berth rooms is an innovation, and should be very popular with this class of passenger. In addition to the staterooms, accommodation is provided for the 164 people in open berths on G deck forward.' *Shipbuilder*, 1911

The accommodation for third-class passengers in these steamers is also of a very superior character, the public rooms being large, airy apartments, suitably furnished, and in excellent positions, and the same applies to the third-class staterooms and berths.' White Star publicity, 1911

LEAVING
BELFAST

DURING the latter part of March 1912, the fitting-out activity on board *Titanic* intensified as the shipyard and the scores of sub-contractors, including interior designers A. Heaton & Co. of London, raced to meet completion deadlines. *Titanic* was scheduled to sail from Belfast on 1 April, but due to strong winds her sea trials and the voyage to Southampton were postponed until the following day. On Monday 2 April 1912, ten months after her launch, *Titanic* was ready for sea.

Although some work in the ship's accommodation was still being finished, the imminent transition of *Titanic* from her birthplace in Belfast to her sailing berth in Southampton was a source of pride for both builders and owners. The officers and crew necessary for the trials and voyage were on board, as were Thomas Andrews of Harland & Wolff and Harold A. Sanderson, a director of the White Star Line. Andrews was accompanied by a number of shipyard men, some of whom were to sail on the ship's maiden voyage to New York. Four Liverpool tugs, brought to Belfast to manoeuvre *Titanic* from her berth at the deepwater fitting-out wharf and then assist the great liner out of the port and down Belfast Lough, were in position by about six o'clock in the morning. After several hours of final preparations on *Titanic*'s bridge and decks, and in her boiler rooms and engine rooms, the departure orders were finally given and slowly the huge vessel was edged away from her berth towards Belfast Lough and the open sea.

Once in the main channel and free of the dockside, *Titanic*'s size and beauty were manifest. With an overall length of 882ft 9in and breadth of 92ft 6in, she measured 46,328 gross tons and so became the largest ship in the world. Like her sister ship, *Titanic* was a triple-screw liner designed for a service speed of 21 knots. The registered horsepower of her engines was 50,000, although the actual power developed was at least 55,000 horsepower. Propelling machinery comprised two sets of four-cylinder triple expansion reciprocating engines, each driving a wing propeller, and a low-pressure turbine driving a centre propeller. This combination arrangement of machinery, pioneered by Harland & Wolff, was designed to obtain increased power without an increase in steam consumption by piping the exhaust steam from the reciprocating engines into the low-pressure turbine. Steam was supplied to the reciprocating engines at 215 p.s.i. by 29 coal-fired boilers, having a total of 159 furnaces. Four enormous funnels, with an average height of 150 feet from the floors of the boiler rooms, towered above *Titanic*'s spacious decks. However, only three funnels were required to take smoke and waste gases from the furnaces. The fourth funnel was in fact a dummy which was placed above the turbine hatch and used as a ventilator. Its incorporation was a required design feature, as four funnels gave an elegant and balanced appearance to the ship, while simultaneously projecting an image of power and magnitude at sea.

∨ *Titanic* was completed, prepared for sea and due to sail on 1 April 1912. However, owing to a strong north-westerly wind, her departure from Belfast was postponed until the following day. This photograph was taken at the deepwater fitting-out wharf on 1 April, as evidenced by the floating crane and the wind-blown smoke from her funnels. (L2696-10)

After one day's trials in the Irish Sea, where the ship's engines and performance were tested, the compasses adjusted and test transmissions made on the Marconi wireless telegraphing system, *Titanic* returned to Belfast at about seven o'clock on the evening of 2 April. Shipyard workers and staff and all others who were not going on to Southampton were taken ashore, while some additional fittings and fresh food were brought on board. The Board of Trade surveyor, Francis Carruthers, signed and dated the ship's certificate 'good for one year from today, 2.4.12'. As representatives of the builders and owners, Thomas Andrews and Harold Sanderson signed the papers signifying *Titanic*'s acceptance by the White Star Line. Andrews had of course been extremely busy throughout the day inspecting and superintending all of the shipboard work necessary for the trials and delivery of *Titanic*. In a brief note to his wife Helen, at home in Comber, County Down, Andrews wrote, 'Just a line to let you know that we got away this morning in fine style and have had a very satisfactory trial. We are getting more ship-shape every hour, but there is still a great deal to be done.'

Shortly after eight o'clock on the evening of 2 April, *Titanic* left Belfast for the last time, now bound for Southampton. During the 570-mile voyage, Andrews was again busy writing reports and working with the shipyard men in completing a myriad of tasks for the smooth running of the ship. Late on Wednesday 3 April, *Titanic* arrived in Southampton and shortly after midnight she was docked without mishap at White Star's transatlantic Berth No. 44. On the next day, Thursday 4 April, Thomas Andrews wrote again to his wife, 'I wired you this morning of our safe arrival after a very satisfactory trip. The weather was good and everyone most pleasant. I think the ship will clean up all right before sailing on Wednesday.' *Titanic*'s maiden voyage from Southampton to New York was scheduled for Wednesday 10 April 1912.

⌄ The beautiful profile of *Titanic* can be seen as she slowly moves
down Belfast Lough towards the open sea, escorted by her tugs,
on 2 April 1912. Her four huge funnels tower more than 80 feet
above the boat deck, while their elegant rake is matched by the
parallel rake of her lofty masts. Their great height ensures that
the Marconi aerial, suspended between them, is at least 50 feet
above the gas and smoke from the funnels. (H1722)

⟨ With a Belfast pilot on the bridge with Captain Smith and guided by four tugs, *Titanic* is carefully taken down the narrow channel of Belfast Lough on 2 April 1912. They are moving very slowly through the calm water, with a light breeze blowing funnel smoke towards the Co. Down shore of the lough. Near the stern of *Titanic*, men are standing on the docking bridge, intended for use when docking or turning in a confined space. The water pumping from *Titanic*'s discharge outlets indicates the working of engines and machinery deep within her hull. The tug *Herculaneum* is keeping station off the starboard side of *Titanic*'s stern. (H1721)

> **DEPARTURE OF THE TITANIC THE WORLD'S LARGEST LINER**
> The new Royal Mail triple-screw steamer *Titanic*, which has been built by Harland & Wolff Ltd, for the White Star Line, left the deepwater wharf shortly after 10 o'clock yesterday morning for Southampton, whence she will sail on her maiden voyage to New York on the 10th inst. The usual scenes of bustle and animation attending the departure of a great liner were witnessed from an early hour in the morning, and as the hawsers were cast off, the *Titanic* – the largest vessel in the world – floated proudly on the water, a monument to the enterprise of her owners and the ingenuity and skill of the eminent firm who built her. She was at once taken in tow by the powerful tugs which were in attendance and the crowds of spectators who had assembled on both sides of the river raised hearty cheers as she was towed into the channel. The mammoth vessel presented an impressive spectacle, looking perfect from keel to truck, while the weather conditions were happily of a favourable character. When the tugs were left behind the compasses were adjusted, after which a satisfactory speed run took place, and the latest triumph of the shipbuilder's art then left for Southampton, carrying with her the best wishes of the citizens of Belfast.' *Belfast News-Letter*, 3 April 1912

Captain Edward J. Smith and his senior officers, April 1912. Left to right, front: James Moody (Sixth Officer), Henry Wilde (Chief Officer), Captain Edward Smith, William Murdoch (First Officer). Back: Hugh McElroy (Chief Purser), Charles Lightoller (Second Officer), Herbert Pitman (Third Officer), Joseph Boxhall (Fourth Officer), Harold Lowe (Fifth Officer). (L4160/9)

' On the boat deck accommodation is provided for the captain and officers, containing smoke-room and mess-room. Rooms for the Marconi installation are also arranged in the same house, with the wheelhouse and navigating bridge adjoining at the fore-end.'
White Star publicity, 1911

Coloured lantern slide of *Titanic* and her escort tugs in Belfast Lough, 2 April 1912 (OMAFP-2010-27-530/2)

'The navigating bridge, from which the vessel is controlled, is situated at the forward end of the boat deck so that the navigating officer may have a clear view ahead. This bridge is a veritable forest of instruments. In the centre is the wheelhouse, containing the telemotor control wheel by which the ship is steered, with a standard compass immediately in front. In front of the wheelhouse are placed the engine-room, docking and steering telegraphs, and loudspeaking telephones to various stations. In the bridge shelter or chart room adjoining are also placed the watertight door controller, the submarine-signal receiver, the helm indicator, the master clocks and other apparatus.' *Shipbuilder*, 1911

∨ Still in the channel of Belfast Lough, *Titanic* dwarfs the escorting tugs, which have been brought over from Liverpool especially for this operation on 2 April 1912. *Huskisson* and *Herculaneum* are positioned astern of *Titanic*, while two more tugs, *Hornby* and *Herald*, are keeping her steady from ahead. Ripples and eddies in the water mark *Titanic*'s stately progress as she slips away from Belfast. Soon the tugs will let her go and *Titanic*'s propellers will churn up the water as she picks up speed and steams out into the open sea for her trials. (H1723)

EMBARKATION

THE new White Star Dock at Southampton, where *Titanic* was moored at Berth No. 44, had been officially inaugurated on 14 June 1911 with the maiden voyage of *Olympic* to New York. Specially built to accommodate the two White Star leviathans, the dock enclosed nearly 16 acres of water to a depth of 40 feet. Passenger and cargo sheds were erected on the concrete quayside adjacent to the liner berths and four enormous cranes travelled on rails alongside to facilitate cargo handling. The London and South Western Railway ran boat trains right to the quayside for the convenience of transatlantic passengers.

From the morning of 4 April 1912 until sailing day, there was ceaseless activity on board *Titanic* to complete outstanding jobs and to make the ship ready for her ocean voyage. The ship's bunkers were filled with an additional 4,427 tons of coal, despite shortages caused by a national coal strike. The crew were signed on in their hundreds, from seamen and stewards to stokers and greasers. They were followed by other shipboard personnel, including postal clerks, restaurant staff and musicians for the ship's orchestra. The ranks of the senior deck officers were modified by the transfer to *Titanic* of *Olympic*'s chief officer, Henry T. Wilde.

In order to complete the passenger facilities, consignments of glassware, cutlery and crockery were supplied to the ship. It was also necessary to provision *Titanic*, and stores were brought on board in huge quantities. Besides a vast supply of refrigerated fresh food, the ship's provisions included 15,000 bottles of beer and 1,000 bottles of wine. A wide variety of general cargo began to arrive for shipment to the United States. Items on the cargo manifest ranged from a motor car to four rolls of linoleum.

During *Titanic*'s week in Southampton, Thomas Andrews was constantly busy superintending completion work, besides showing parties around the ship and having endless discussions with officials, agents, sub-contractors, ship's officers and White Star managers. His temporary secretary later wrote, 'Through the various days that the vessel lay at Southampton, Mr Andrews was never idle. He generally left his hotel about 8.30 for the offices, where he dealt with his correspondence, then went on board until 6.30 ... He would himself put in their place such things as racks, tables, chairs, berth ladders, electric fans, saying that except he saw everything right he would not be satisfied.' By 9 April, Easter Tuesday, the frantic preparations for *Titanic*'s maiden voyage were almost finished. That evening, in a letter home to his wife, Thomas Andrews quietly confided his pride in the great ship, 'The *Titanic* is now complete and will I think do the old firm credit to-morrow when we sail.'

The following day, Wednesday 10 April 1912, *Titanic*, under the command of Captain Edward J. Smith, RD, RNR, was ready to sail on her maiden voyage to New York. From 9.30 in the morning large numbers of second- and third-class passengers boarded the ship, following the arrival of the early boat train from London. Two hours later, about 11.30, many first-class passengers arrived on a special London boat train and boarded *Titanic* within thirty minutes of her sailing time. Prominent wealthy American passengers included Mr & Mrs John J. Astor, whose first-class ticket cost just over £224.

∨ *Titanic* moored at Berth No. 44, White Star Dock,
Southampton. *c.*6 April 1912. The large quayside
crane, travelling on rails, is loading materials on
board the ship. (Courtney #5)

Just before midday a mighty blast on *Titanic's* huge whistles signalled the imminent departure of the ship. Amidst clouds of smoke and steam, the mooring lines were cast off and tugs began to manoeuvre *Titanic* away from her berth and out of the dock, before swinging her through a 90-degree turn in the River Test. Now facing downstream, *Titanic* began to move ahead. Within a short distance, a collision with the liner *New York* was narrowly averted when her mooring lines snapped as a result of the turbulence caused by *Titanic's* propellers. After an hour's delay *Titanic* got under way again and soon she was steaming down Southampton Water towards the English Channel, bound first for the French port of Cherbourg and then Queenstown in Ireland, before heading out into the Atlantic for New York.

'... But up where we were – some 60 feet above the waterline – there was no indication of the strength of the tossing swell below. This indeed is the one great impression I received from my first trip on the *Titanic* – and everyone with whom I spoke shared it – her wonderful steadiness. Were it not for the brisk breeze blowing along the decks one would have scarcely imagined that every hour found us some 20 knots farther upon our course ...

The lordly contempt of the *Titanic* for anything less than a hurricane seemed most marvellous and comforting. But other things besides her steadiness filled us with wonder. Deck over deck and apartment after apartment lent their deceitful aid to persuade us that instead of being on the sea we were still on terra firma ... After dinner as we sat in the beautiful lounge listening to the White Star orchestra playing the "Tales of Hoffman" and "Cavalleria Rusticana" selection more than once we heard the remark: "You would never imagine you were on board a ship". Still harder was it to believe that up on the top deck it was blowing a gale ...

Lifts and lounges and libraries are not generally associated in the public mind with second class, yet in the Titanic all are found. It needed the assurance of our guide that we had left the saloon and were really in the second class.

On the crowded third-class deck were hundreds of English, Dutch, Italian and French mingling in happy fellowship, and when we wandered down among them we found that for them, too, the *Titanic* was a wonder. No more general cabins, but hundreds of comfortable rooms, with two, four or six berths each, beautifully covered in red-and-white coverlets. Here, too, are lounges and smoking rooms, less magnificent than those amidships, to be sure, but nonetheless comfortable, and which, with the swivel chairs and separate tables in the dining rooms, struck me as not quite fitting in with my previous notion of steerage accommodation ...

And then this morning, when the full Atlantic swell came upon our port side, so stately and measured was the roll of the mighty ship that one needed to compare the moving of the side with the steady line of the clear horizon.' A first-class passenger's account of *Titanic's* voyage from Southampton to Queenstown, *Belfast Evening Telegraph*, 15 April 1912

'Excellent accommodation for the firemen has been provided at the forward end of the vessel, through the lower, middle, upper and saloon decks, giving access to the boiler rooms by two spiral stairs and tunnel. The arrangement keeps the firemen entirely clear of the passenger accommodation.'
White Star publicity, 1911

The unusual lack of activity in this photograph of *Titanic* at her Southampton berth suggests it was taken on Easter Sunday, 7 April 1912. (Courtney #1)

In this wonderfully atmospheric photograph, *Titanic* is being manoeuvred away from Berth No. 44 to begin her maiden voyage on 10 April 1912. The old man in the foreground is a perfect foil for the great ship and the hopes of all on board. (Courtney #6)

∧ Attendant tugs have manoeuvred *Titanic* through
a 90-degree turn in the River Test so that she now
heads downstream to leave Southampton. The man
in the foreground, holding a camera, is watching the
operation from the same ship as the photographer,
10 April 1912. (Courtney #7)

❛ The working arrangements on board the
Olympic and *Titanic* are necessarily on
a scale in keeping with the great size of the
vessels. The number of crew employed on
board each ship for all purposes is about 860.
Of these about 65 belong to the navigating
department, 320 are employed in the
engineers' department, and 475 are engaged
in the stewards' and catering department.'
Shipbuilder, 1911

' Among the passengers are Mr Bruce Ismay and a number of well-known Americans. A large concourse of people had gathered to speed the vessel on her maiden voyage, and she made an impressive spectacle as she quietly glided in brilliant sunshine down Southampton Water, quite dwarfing all the adjacent shipping.'
Belfast News-Letter, 11 April 1912

∧ Now the tugs have dropped their lines, *Titanic* is beginning to move downstream under her own power. Her size, beauty and elegance contrast with the functionality of the attendant tugs, 10 April 1912. (Courtney #9)

∧ A dramatic photograph of a near collision at Southampton between the departing *Titanic* and the liner *New York*. *Titanic*'s increasing speed and propeller turbulence caused *New York*'s mooring lines to snap and her stern began to swing out towards *Titanic*. The quick actions of Captain Smith, Pilot Bowyer and Captain Gale of the tug Vulcan prevented the two ships colliding, although *New York* drifted to within four feet of *Titanic*'s hull. Had a collision occurred, *Titanic* would not have sailed that day and would not have converged with the iceberg.

∧ *Titanic* steams away from Southampton, 10 April
1912. Eerily, the broken glass plate negative has
cracked the ship close to the position where
Titanic struck the iceberg five days after this
photograph was taken. (Courtney #3)

A SECTION DRAWING OF

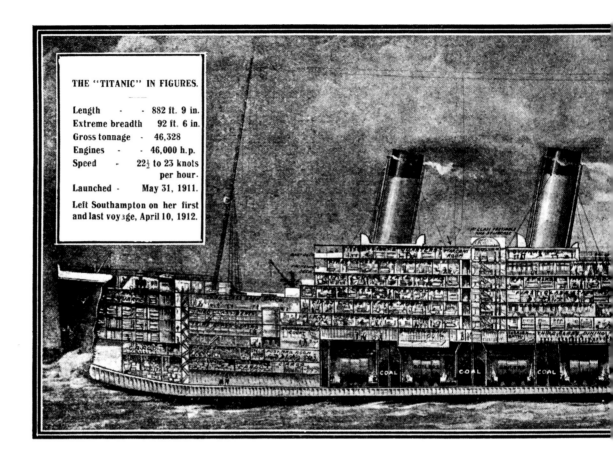

THE "TITANIC" IN FIGURES.

Length	- - 882 ft. 9 in.
Extreme breadth	92 ft. 6 in.
Gross tonnage	- 46,328
Engines	- - 46,000 h.p.
Speed	- 22½ to 23 knots per hour.
Launched	- May 31, 1911.

Left Southampton on her first and last voyage, April 10, 1912.

THE "TITANIC'S" LARDER.

The "Titanic" took on board at Southampton just before she sailed :

Fresh Meat (lbs.)	... 75,000	Potatoes (tons)	... ...	40
Poultry (lbs.)	. 25,000	Ale and Stout (bottles)	...	15,000
Fresh Eggs	... 35,000	Minerals (bottles)	...	12,000
Cereals (lbs.)	... 10,000	Wines (bottles)	...	1,000
Flour (barrels)	... 250	Electroplate (pieces)	...	26,000
Tea (lbs.)	... 1,000	Chinaware (pieces)	...	25,000
Fresh Milk (gals.)	... 1,500	Plates and Dishes (pieces)		21,000
Fresh Cream (qts.)	... 1,200	Glass (pieces)	...	7,000
Sugar (tons)	... 5	Cutlery (pieces)	...	5,000

PREVIOUS GREA

Following are some of the principal

1911.—September 20 : Olympic (Captain Smith in command collision with H.M.S. Cruiser Hawke in Cowes Road
1910.—February 9 : French steamer General Chanzy wrecke Minorca... ... ...
1909.—January 23 : Italian steamer Florida in collision with White Star liner Republic, about 170 miles east of York, during fog. Large number of lives saved by arrival of the Baltic, which received a distress signal up by wireless from the Republic. The Republic s while being towed to harbour ... ...
1908.—March 23 : Japanese steamer Mutsu Maru sunk in lision near Hakodate ... ...
1907.—February 21 : G.E.R. steamer Berlin wrecked off H of Holland during gale
1906.—August 4 : Italian emigrant ship Sirio, bound for So America, struck a rock off Cape Palos ... ...
1905.—November 19 : L.S.W.R. steamer Hilda struck on a near St. Malo and became a total loss ... ...
1904.—June 15 : General Slocum, American excursion stea caught fire at Long Island Sound ... ...

∧ 'The Deathless Story of the *Titanic*',
Lloyd's Weekly News, 1912

GIANT LINER "TITANIC."

THE "TITANIC" IN FIGURES.

Lifeboats carried - - 16
Collapsible boats - - 4
Capacity of each lifeboat 50 persons.
Life preservers on board sufficient for all.
Number of passengers "Titanic" could carry 3,500
Number carried at time of disaster - - 1,400
Crew - - - 940

NG DISASTERS.

that have occurred in recent years :

	Lives Lost
ay 6 : Govermorta lost in cyclone, Bay of Bengal ...	739
pril 1 : Aslan, Turkish Transport, wrecked in the Red ea	180
arch 30 : Stella, wrecked off Casquets	105
ctober 14 : Mohegan, Atlantic Transport Co. steamer, recked on the Manacles	107
ecember 7 : Salier, North German Lloyd steamer, recked off Cape Corrubebo, N. Spain	281
e 16 : Drummond Castle, wrecked off Ushant	247
nuary 30 : Elbe, North German Lloyd steamer, from emen to New York, sunk in collision with the Crathie, Aberdeen, off Lowestoft	334
ne 22 : H.M.S. Victoria, sunk after collision with .M.S. Camperdown	359
arch 24 : H.M.S. Eurydice, wrecked off Dunnose eadland, Isle of Wight	300
bruary 26 : Troopship Birkenhead struck upon a ck off Simon's Bay, South Africa. The heroism displayed by the men on board has earned them undying nown	454

THE WORLD'S LARGEST SHIPS.

	Gross Tonnage.		Length, feet.		Breadth, feet.		Speed, knots.
*GIGANTIC ...	50,000	...	1,000	...	112	...	—
*AQUITANIA ...	50,000	...	910	...	95	...	23
*IMPERATOR ...	50,000	...	910	...	95½	...	22
TITANIC ..	46,328	...	883	...	92·6	...	22½
OLYMPIC ...	45,324	...	883	...	92·6	...	22½
MAURETANIA ...	31,938	...	762	...	88	...	25
LUSITANIA ...	31,550	...	762	...	87	...	25

* Building or projected.

Triple-Screw R.M.S., "OLYMPIC,"

45,324 Tons

The Largest Steamer in the World.

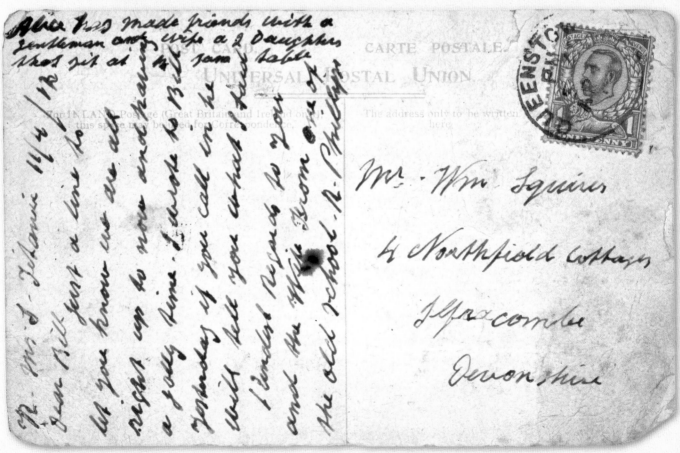

R.M.S. Titanic 16/4/12

Dear Bill just a line to let you know we are all right up to now and having a jolly time. I wrote to Bill yesterday if you call in he will tell you what I said. Kindest Regards to you all and the Wife from one of the old school. R. Phillips

Alice has made friends with a gentleman and wife & 2 Daughters that sit at the same table

POST CARD.   CARTE POSTALE.

UNIVERSAL POSTAL UNION.

For INLAND Postage (Great Britain and Ireland only) this space may be used for Correspondence.

The address only to be written here.

Mr. Wm. Squires

4 Northfield Cottages

Ilfracombe

Devonshire

Pages from a letter written on board *Titanic* by Mr Herbert Denbury, a passenger in second class. The letter is incorrectly dated 10 April 1912, as *Titanic* did not arrive in Queenstown until 11 April. Mr Denbury lost his life in the disaster. (TR60-1/2)

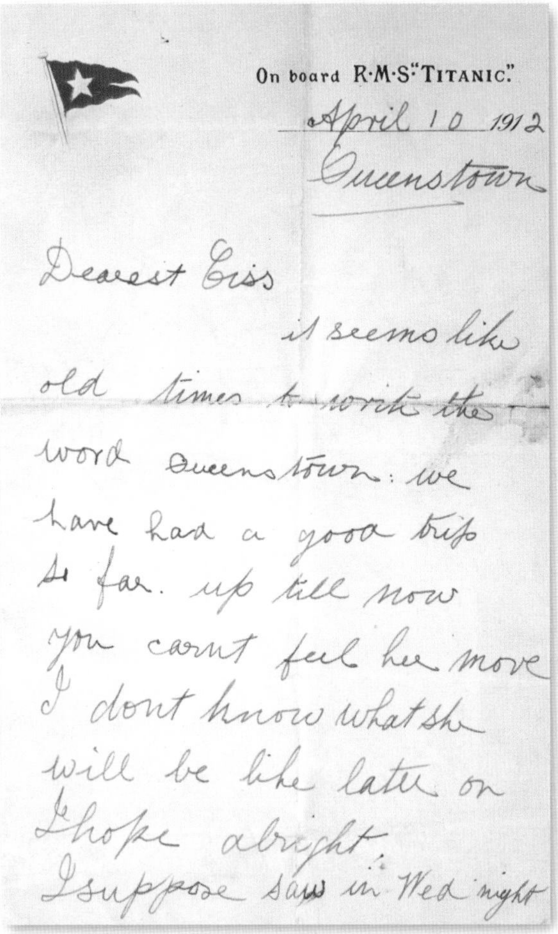

White Star Line postcard projecting the magnitude and power of *Olympic* and *Titanic*. This card was posted on board *Titanic* at Queenstown (Cobh), Co. Cork, the ship's last port of call before she sailed out into the Atlantic on 11 April 1912. It was written by Mr Robert Phillips, travelling in second class with his daughter Alice. Mr Phillips lost his life in the disaster, though his daughter was saved. (TR198-10)

On board R·M·S· "Titanic."

April 10 1912
Queenstown

Dearest Ciss

it seems like old times to write the word Queenstown. we have had a good trip so far. up till now you carnt feel her move I dont know what she will be like latter on I hope alright. I suppose saw in Wed night

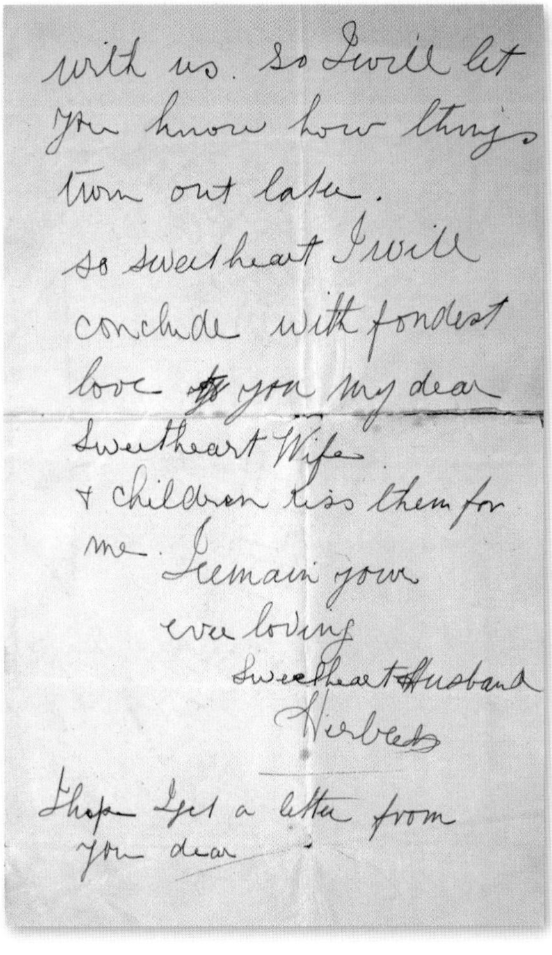

with us. so I will let you know how things turn out later.
So sweetheart I will conclude with fondest love to you my dear Sweetheart Wife & children kiss them for me. I remain your ever loving Sweetheart Husband Herbert

I hope I get a letter from you dear

14

'WE ARE ON THE ICE'

TITANIC left the Irish port of Queenstown on the afternoon of Thursday 11 April 1912, with 2,201 souls on board. Although the twenty lifeboats carried by the ship exceeded the number required by Board of Trade regulations, they actually only had space for 1,178 people. Steaming into the Atlantic, *Titanic* set course for the accepted outward-bound route for mail steamers at that time of year. Usually called the Outward Southern Track, it followed the arc of a great circle from the Fastnet Light, off the south-west coast of Ireland, to the Nantucket Shoal light vessel, off the coast of the United States, and from there on to New York. Three days later at 9 a.m. on Sunday 14 April (*Titanic* time), a wireless message from SS *Caronia* was received by Captain Smith:

CAPTAIN. *TITANIC* – WEST-BOUND STEAMERS REPORT BERGS, GROWLERS AND FIELD ICE IN 42° N. FROM 49° TO 51° W., 12TH APRIL. COMPLIMENTS – BARR.

In the course of the day and evening several other ice messages were received in *Titanic*'s Marconi room. At 9.40 p.m. SS *Mesaba* transmitted another warning:

FROM *MESABA* TO *TITANIC* AND ALL EAST-BOUND SHIPS. ICE REPORT IN LAT. 42° 25' N., LONG. 49° TO LONG. 50° 30' W. SAW MUCH HEAVY PACK ICE AND GREAT NUMBER LARGE ICEBERGS. ALSO FIELD ICE. WEATHER GOOD, CLEAR.

This message clearly indicated the presence of ice in the immediate vicinity of *Titanic*, but unfortunately it was not delivered to the Master or any of the officers. The Marconi operator was very busy from 8 p.m. onwards transmitting passengers' messages via Cape Race, Newfoundland and, failing to grasp the importance of the message, he set it aside until he was less busy. Nevertheless, by Sunday evening Captain Smith and his officers knew that the ship was entering a region where ice might be expected. Despite this, *Titanic*'s speed was not reduced and at 10 p.m. she was registering 45 knots every two hours by the Cherub log. The weather was clear and fine, and although there was no moon the stars were out.

At 11.40 p.m. one of the look-outs in the crow's-nest struck three blows on the gong, which was the accepted warning for something ahead, following this immediately afterwards by a telephone message to the bridge 'Iceberg right ahead'. Almost simultaneously with the three-gong signal Mr Murdoch, the officer of the watch, gave the order 'Hard-a-starboard' and immediately telegraphed down to the engine room, 'Stop. Full speed astern'. The helm was already hard over and the ship's head had fallen off about two points to port, when she collided with an iceberg well forward on her starboard side. Mr Murdoch at the same time pulled the lever over which closed the watertight doors in the engine and boiler rooms. The Master rushed out on to the bridge and asked Mr Murdoch what the ship had struck. Mr Murdoch replied, 'An iceberg, Sir. I hard-a-starboarded and reversed the engines, and I was going to hard-a-port round it but she was too close. I could not do any more. I have closed the watertight doors.' *Mersey Report on the Loss of the Steamship Titanic*, 1912

Titanic was travelling at over twenty knots when she struck, and in less than ten seconds her hull was opened below the waterline on the starboard side for a length of 300 feet. The fore peak, No. 1 hold, No. 2 hold, No. 3 hold, No. 6 boiler room and No. 5 boiler room were immediately open to the sea about five feet above the watertight inner bottom. Water entered No. 5 boiler room at a rate equal to the stream of a fire hose and was within the capacity of the pumps. Damage to the hull at the five forward compartments was much more severe and within ten minutes they were flooded to a height of fourteen feet above the keel. This was a rate of inflow with which the ship's pumps could not possibly cope. *Titanic*'s design and arrangement of transverse watertight bulkheads permitted her to float in safety with any two compartments flooded, and it would have been possible for her to remain afloat even with four compartments flooded. She could not, however, float with the four forward compartments and the forward boiler room (No. 6) flooded. Because of the limited height of *Titanic*'s watertight bulkheads, and because the decks above them were not watertight, it was inevitable that she would sink by the head as water flowed from compartment to compartment over the top of each watertight bulkhead. The enormous inrush of water to the five forward compartments doomed the ship.

The collision occurred at 11.40 p.m. (ship's time) and it took some twenty minutes for it to be realised that *Titanic* could not live. About 12.05 a.m. the order was given to uncover the lifeboats under davits and the work began on both sides of the ship under the superintendence of five officers. At 12.20 a.m. the boats were swung out, although there were few passengers on deck at this time. The noise of steam blowing off was so great that voices could not be heard and Mr Lightoller, Second Officer, had to give directions with his hands. Meanwhile stewards had been rousing passengers, helping them with their lifebelts and getting them up to the boat deck. At about 12.30 a.m. the order was given to place women and children in the lifeboats and fifteen minutes later the boats began to be lowered to the water sixty-five feet below. For various reasons not all the boats were filled to their carrying capacity. Passengers were reluctant to leave the ship, thinking that the risk was less than in the boats. Some women were frightened of the long descent to the sea and some refused to leave their husbands. The hope of imminent rescue made passengers still more unwilling to leave *Titanic*:

TITANIC Icon of an Age

> These boats left behind them many hundreds of lives to perish ... It is to be remembered that the night was dark, the noise of the escaping steam was terrifying, the peril, though perhaps not generally recognised, was imminent and great, and many passengers who were unable to speak or to understand English were being collected together and hurried into the boats. *Mersey Report on the Loss of the Steamship Titanic*, 1912

After the last of the eighteen boats, lowered from the davits, left the ship, water came up the stairway under the boat deck almost immediately. Two remaining lifeboats floated off the ship and were subsequently utilised as rafts.

About 12.45 a.m., when the first boat was lowered, Mr Boxall, Fourth Officer, began to fire distress-signal rockets from the boat deck. They exploded in the air, throwing off white stars, and their firing continued until Boxall left the ship about 1.45 a.m. He also used a Morse light from the bridge in the direction of a ship whose lights he saw five or six miles off. He got no answer.

When the sinking condition of the ship was realised, Captain Smith ordered wireless messages to be sent out to all steamers within reach. At 12.15 a.m. the first distress signal CQD was transmitted by *Titanic*.

Form No. **4.—100**— 17.8.10.   Deld. Date **14 Apr 1912**

The Marconi International Marine Communication Co., Ltd.,
WATERGATE HOUSE, YORK BUILDINGS, ADELPHI, LONDON, W.C.

No. **"OLYMPIC"**   OFFICE. **14 Apr**   19 **12**

CHARGES TO PAY.

Handed in at **TITANIC**

This message has been transmitted subject to the conditions printed on the back hereof, which have been agreed to by the Sender. If the accuracy of this message be doubted, the Receiver, on paying the necessary charges, may have it repeated whenever possible, from Office to Office over the Company's system, and should any error be shown to exist, all charges for such repetition will be refunded. This Form must accompany any enquiry respecting this Telegram.

Total

To   OLYMPIC

Eleven pm NEW YORK TIME TITANIC SENDING OUT SIGNALS OF DISTRESS ANSWERED HIS CALLS.

TITANIC REPLIES AND GIVES ME HIS POSITION 41.46 N 50 14 W AND SAYS "WE HAVE STRUCK AN ICE BERG".

OUR DISTANCE FROM TITANIC 505 MILES.

Marconigram #1

SOME FACTS OF THE DISASTER.

The iceberg, from 50 to 100 feet high, was struck at 11.35 p.m.

The blow was a glancing one on the starboard side, which was ripped open, rendering useless the essential water-tight compartments.

The "Titanic" sank in two miles of water, two hours and forty-five minutes after she struck.

Jack Phillips, the "Titanic's" wireless operator, remained at his post flashing out signals for assistance until the deck was awash.

Captain Smith, indifferent to his own safety, worked till the very last moment to save as many as possible. "Be British" was his word to one and all.

The "Carpathia's" wireless operator, by a lucky chance, was up late, and heard the "Titanic's" call for help.

The White Star liner "Olympic," on hearing the "Titanic's" wireless call for assistance, covered 400 miles at twenty-four knots, the highest speed the liner has ever attained.

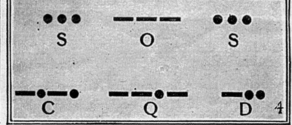

How the wireless call for help was sent.

(1.) Jack Phillips, the chief Marconi operator on the "Titanic," who flashed out his messages till the ship went down.

(2.) The wireless cabin on an ocean liner, the operator receiving a message.

(3.) Harold Bride, the second Marconi operator on the "Titanic," who was saved.

(4.) The wireless signal of distress, "S. O. S." in the Morse code. Formerly the signal "C. Q. D." was used.

Titanic's two wireless operators, Jack Phillips (lost) and Harold Bride (saved), were employees of The Marconi International Marine Communication Co. Ltd. They stayed at their posts until the end. The distress signal CQD was transmitted by Titanic at 12.15 a.m., changing to SOS at 12.45 a.m., while also continuing with CQD.

The plight of the ship and all those on board is vividly documented in the following edited
record of the Marconigrams transmitted and received between 12.15 a.m. and 2.17 a.m. when
Titanic's signals abruptly ended:

TITANIC TIME (A.M.)

12.15   LA PROVENCE RECEIVES TITANIC DISTRESS SIGNALS.

12.15   MOUNT TEMPLE HEARD TITANIC SENDING C.Q.D. SAYS REQUIRE
          ASSISTANCE. GIVES POSITION. CANNOT HEAR ME. ADVISE MY
          CAPTAIN HIS POSITION 41.46 N., 50.24 W

12.18   YPIRANGA HEARS C.Q.D. FROM TITANIC. POSITION 41.44 N.,
          50.24 W. REQUIRE ASSISTANCE (CALLS ABOUT 10 TIMES).

12.25   C.Q.D. CALL RECEIVED FROM TITANIC BY CARPATHIA. TITANIC
          SAID, 'COME AT ONCE. WE HAVE STRUCK A BERG. IT'S A
          C.Q.D.O.M. POSITION 41.46 N., 50.14 W'

12.26   M.G.Y. (I.E. TITANIC) SAYS C.Q.D. HERE CORRECTED POSITION
          41.46 N., 50.14 W. REQUIRE IMMEDIATE ASSISTANCE. WE HAVE
          COLLISION WITH ICEBERG. SINKING. CAN NOTHING HEAR FOR
          NOISE OF STEAM. SENT ABOUT 15 TO 20 TIMES TO YPIRANGA.

12.27   TITANIC SENDS FOLLOWING: 'I REQUIRE ASSISTANCE
          IMMEDIATELY. STRUCK BY ICEBERG IN 41.46 N., 50.14 W'

12.30   TITANIC GIVES HIS POSITION TO FRANKFURT AND SAYS, 'TELL
          YOUR CAPTAIN TO COME TO OUR HELP. WE ARE ON THE ICE.'

12.30   MOUNT TEMPLE HEARS M.G.Y. (TITANIC) STILL CALLING C.Q.D.
          OUR CAPTAIN REVERSES SHIP. WE ARE ABOUT 50 MILES OFF.

12.45   TITANIC CALLS OLYMPIC S.O.S. [THIS WAS ONE OF THE FIRST
          OCCASIONS THE NOW FAMILIAR CALL WAS SENT OUT BY A SHIP
          IN DISTRESS.]

12.50   TITANIC CALLS C.Q.D. AND SAYS 'I REQUIRE IMMEDIATE
          ASSISTANCE. POSITION 41.46 N., 50.14 W.' RECEIVED
          BY CELTIC.

1.02	TITANIC CALLS ASIAN AND SAID 'WANT IMMEDIATE ASSISTANCE'.

1.02   TITANIC CALLS ASIAN AND SAID 'WANT IMMEDIATE ASSISTANCE'.

1.10   TITANIC TO M.K.C. (OLYMPIC). 'WE ARE IN COLLISION WITH BERG. SINKING HEAD DOWN. 41.46 N., 50.14 W. COME AS SOON AS POSSIBLE. CAPTAIN SAYS GET YOUR BOATS READY. WHAT IS YOUR POSITION.'

1.25   OLYMPIC SENDS POSITION TO TITANIC 40.52 N., 61.18 W. 'ARE YOU STEERING SOUTHERLY TO MEET US?' TITANIC REPLIES, 'WE ARE PUTTING THE WOMEN OFF IN THE BOATS'.

1.35   OLYMPIC ASKS TITANIC WHAT WEATHER HE HAD. TITANIC REPLIES 'CLEAR AND CALM'.

1.35   BALTIC HEARS TITANIC SAY 'ENGINE ROOM GETTING FLOODED'.

1.37   BALTIC TELLS TITANIC, 'WE ARE RUSHING TO YOU'.

1.40   OLYMPIC TO TITANIC, 'AM LIGHTING UP ALL POSSIBLE BOILERS AS FAST AS CAN'.

1.40   CAPE RACE SAYS TO VIRGINIAN, 'PLEASE TELL YOUR CAPTAIN THIS: THE OLYMPIC IS MAKING ALL SPEED FOR TITANIC, BUT HIS [OLYMPIC'S] POSITION IS 40.32 N., 61.18 W. YOU ARE MUCH NEARER TO TITANIC. THE TITANIC IS ALREADY PUTTING WOMEN OFF IN THE BOATS, AND HE SAYS THE WEATHER THERE IS CALM AND CLEAR. THE OLYMPIC IS THE ONLY SHIP WE HAVE HEARD SAY, GOING TO THE ASSISTANCE OF THE TITANIC. THE OTHERS MUST BE A LONG WAY FROM THE TITANIC.'

1.45   LAST SIGNALS HEARD FROM TITANIC BY CARPATHIA. 'ENGINE ROOM FULL UP TO BOILERS.'

1.48   ASIAN HEARD TITANIC CALL S.O.S. ASIAN ANSWERS TITANIC BUT RECEIVES NO ANSWER.

2.00   VIRGINIAN HEARS TITANIC CALLING VERY FAINTLY, HIS POWER BEING GREATLY REDUCED.

2.17   VIRGINIAN HEARS TITANIC CALL C.Q., BUT UNABLE TO READ HIM. TITANIC'S SIGNALS END VERY ABRUPTLY AS POWER SUDDENLY SWITCHED OFF.

2.20   THIS WAS THE OFFICIAL TIME THE TITANIC FOUNDERED IN 41.46 N., 50.14 W. AS GIVEN BY THE CARPATHIA IN MESSAGE TO THE OLYMPIC.

∧ *Mersey Report on the Loss of the Steamship Titanic,* 1912

Form No. **4.**—**100**— 17.8.10.

Deld. Date __14 APR 1912__

The Marconi International Marine Communication Co., Ltd.,

WATERGATE HOUSE, YORK BUILDINGS, ADELPHI, LONDON, W.C.

No. __OLYMPIC__ OFFICE. __14 Apr__ 19 __12__

Handed in at __TITANIC__

CHARGES TO PAY.

This message has been transmitted subject to the conditions printed on the back hereof, which have been agreed to by the Sender. If the accuracy of this message be doubted, the Receiver, on paying the necessary charges, may have it repeated whenever possible, from Office to Office over the Company's system, and should any error be shown to exist, all charges for such repetition will be refunded. This Form must accompany any enquiry respecting this Telegram.

Total

To

11.20 PM N.Y.T. EXCHANGED SIGNALS WITH THE TITANIC. HE SAYS

TELL CAPTAIN GET YOUR BOATS READY AND WHAT IS YOUR POSITION.

Form No. **4.**—**100**— 17.8.10.

Deld. Date __14 APR 1912__

The Marconi International Marine Communication Co., Ltd.,

WATERGATE HOUSE, YORK BUILDINGS, ADELPHI, LONDON, W.C.

No. __OLYMPIC.__ OFFICE. __14 APR 1912__ 19 __

Handed in at __TITANIC__

CHARGES TO PAY.

This message has been transmitted subject to the conditions printed on the back hereof, which have been agreed to by the Sender. If the accuracy of this message be doubted, the Receiver, on paying the necessary charges, may have it repeated whenever possible, from Office to Office over the Company's system, and should any error be shown to exist, all charges for such repetition will be refunded. This Form must accompany any enquiry respecting this Telegram.

Total

To

11.40 PM. N.Y.T. TITANIC SAYS TELL CAPTAIN WE ARE PUTTING THE

PASSENGERS OFF IN SMALL BOATS.

11.45 PM. N.Y.T. ASKED THE TITANIC WHAT WEATHER HE HAD

HE SAYS CLEAR AND CALM.

Sent date __14 APR 1912__

The Marconi International Marine Communication Company, Ltd.

WATERGATE HOUSE, YORK BUILDINGS, ADELPHI. LONDON, W.C.

No. __OLYMPIC.__ _____OFFICE __14 APR 1912__ _____19___

Prefix _____ Code _____ Words_____

Office of Origin __OLYMPIC.__

Service Instructions : _____

CHARGES TO PAY.		
Marconi Charge ...		
Other Line Charge...		
Delivery Charge ...		
Total . . .		
Office sent to	Time sent	By whom sent
	m.	

__SENT TO TITANIC AT 11.50 PM N. Y. T.__

READ THE CONDITIONS PRINTED ON THE BACK OF THE FORM.

To : COMMANDER TITANIC

AM	LIGHTING	UP	ALL	POSSIBLE
BOILERS	AS	FAST	AS	CAN.
			HADDOCK	

(This was our last communication with the Titanic)

Coningham Bros., Printers, etc., Limehouse. E.

Marconigram #4

Deld. Date __15 APR 1912__

The Marconi International Marine Communication Co., Ltd.,

WATERGATE HOUSE, YORK BUILDINGS, ADELPHI, LONDON, W.C.

No. __OLYMPIC.__ _____OFFICE. __15 APR 1912__ ____19___

CARPATHIA

Handed in at _____

This message has been transmitted subject to the conditions printed on the back hereof, which have been agreed to by the Sender. If the accuracy of this message be doubted, the Receiver, on paying the necessary charges, may have it repeated whenever possible, from Office to Office over the Company's system, and should any error be shown to exist, all charges for such repetition will be refunded. This Form must accompany any enquiry respecting this Telegram.

CHARGES TO PAY.		
Total		

To OLYMPIC Received 2.10 pm N.Y.T.

WE RECEIVED DISTRESS SIGNAL CALL FROM THE TITANIC AT ELEVEN TWENTY AND PROCEEDED RIGHT TO SPOT MENTIONED. ON ARRIVAL AT DAYBREAK WE SAW ICE 25 MILES LONG APPARENTLY SOLID, QUANTITY OF WRECKAGE AND NUMBER OF BOATS FULL OF LIVES. WE RAISED ABOUT SIX HUNDRED AND SEVENTY SOULS. TITANIC HAS SUNK SHE WENT DOWN IN TWO HOURS. CAPTAIN AND ALL ENGINEERS OUR CAPTAIN SENT ORDER THAT THERE WAS NO NEED FOR BALTIC TO COME ANY FURTHER SO WITH THAT SHE RETURNED ON HER COURSE TO LIVERPOOL. WE HAVE TWO OR THREE OFFICERS ABOARD AND THE SECOND MARCONI OPERATOR WHO HAD BEEN CREEPING HIS WAY THROUGH WATER AT 30 DEGREES FOR SEVERAL HOURS. MR. ISMAY IS ABOARD.

Marconigram #5

Form No. 4.—100.—17.8.10.

Deld. Date **15 APR 1912**

The Marconi International Marine Communication Co., Ltd.,

WATERGATE HOUSE, YORK BUILDINGS, ADELPHI, LONDON, W.C.

No. **OLYMPIC.**   OFFICE. **15 APR 1912** _____ 19 ____

Handed in at **CARPATHIA**

	CHARGES TO PAY.		
This message has been transmitted subject to the conditions printed on the back hereof, which have been agreed to by the Sender. If the accuracy of this message be doubted, the Receiver, on paying the necessary charges, may have it repeated whenever possible, from Office to Office over the Company's system, and should any error be shown to exist, all charges for such repetition will be refunded. This Form must accompany any enquiry respecting this Telegram.			
	Total		

To

COMMANDER OLYMPIC. RECEIVED 3.18 PM N.Y.T.

MR. BRUCE ISMAY IS UNDER AN OPIATE.

ROSTRON.

Form No. 4.—100.—17.8.10.

Deld. Date **15 APR 1912**

The Marconi International Marine Communication Co., Ltd.,

WATERGATE HOUSE, YORK BUILDINGS, ADELPHI, LONDON, W.C.

No. **OLYMPIC.**   OFFICE. **15 APR 1912** _____ 19 ____

Handed in at **CARPATHIA**

	CHARGES TO PAY.		
This message has been transmitted subject to the conditions printed on the back hereof, which have been agreed to by the Sender. If the accuracy of this message be doubted, the Receiver, on paying the necessary charges, may have it repeated whenever possible, from Office to Office over the Company's system, and should any error be shown to exist, all charges for such repetition will be refunded. This Form must accompany any enquiry respecting this Telegram.			
	Total		

To

COMMANDER O L Y M P I C   RECEIVED 3.20 pm NYT

DO YOU THINK IT IS ADVISABLE TITANIC'S PASSENGERS SEE OLYMPIC.
PERSONALLY I SAY NOT. ROSTRON.

Form No. 4.—100.—17.8.10.   Deld. Date 15 APR 1912

The Marconi International Marine Communication Co., Ltd.,
WATERGATE HOUSE, YORK BUILDINGS, ADELPHI, LONDON, W.C.

No. OLYMPIC.   OFFICE.   15 APR 1912   19

Handed in at   CARPATHIA

	CHARGES TO PAY.
This message has been transmitted subject to the conditions printed on the back hereof, which have been agreed to by the Sender. If the accuracy of this message be doubted, the Receiver, on paying the necessary charges, may have it repeated whenever possible, from Office to Office over the Company's system, and should any error be shown to exist, all charges for such repetition will be refunded. This Form must accompany any enquiry respecting this Telegram.	Total

To   COMMANDER OLYMPIC   RECEIVED 3.22 pm NYT

MR. ISMAY ORDERS OLYMPIC NOT TO BE SEEN BY CARPATHIA.

NO TRANSFER TO TAKE PLACE. ROSTRON.

Form No. 1.—100.—17.11.11.   Sent date 15 APR 1912

The Marconi International Marine Communication Company, Ltd.
WATERGATE HOUSE, YORK BUILDINGS, ADELPHI, LONDON, W.C.

No. / OLYMPIC.   OFFICE   15 APR 1912   19

Prefix _____ Code _____ Words _____

Office of Origin   OLYMPIC.

Service Instructions : _____

SENT TO CAPE RACE AT 4.35 pm EST

CHARGES TO PAY.		
Marconi Charge ...		
Other Line Charge...		
Delivery Charge ...		
Total . . .		
Office sent to	Time sent	By whom sent
	m.	

READ THE CONDITIONS PRINTED ON THE BACK OF THE FORM.

To :   ISMAY NEW YORK AND LIVERPOOL.

CARPATHIA REACHED TITANIC POSITION AT DAYBREAK FOUND BOATS AND WRECKAGE ONLY TITANIC HAD FOUNDERED ABOUT 2.20am IN 41.16 N 50.14 W ALL HER BOATS ACCOUNTED FOR ABOUT 675 SOULS SAVED CREW AND PASSENGERS LATTER NEARLY ALL WOMEN AND CHILDREN LEYLAND LINE SS CALIFORNIAN REMAINING AND SEARCHING POSITION OF DISASTER CARPATHIA RETURNING TO NEWYORK WITH SURVIVORS PLEASE INFORM CUNARD.

HADDOCK.

CONINGHAM BROS., Printers, etc., Limehouse, E.

PLEASE ASK FOR OFFICIAL RECEIPT.
Code Addresses registered only with Cable Companies are not available for messages through British Post Office Stations.

Marconigram #15

233

Titanic's Second Officer, Mr Lightoller remained on board the ship until near the end. According to his account, she:

> seemed to take a dive and he just walked into the water. When he came to the surface all her funnels were above the water. Her stern was gradually rising out of the water and the propellers were clear of the water. The ship did not break in two: and she did eventually attain the perpendicular, when the second funnel from aft about reached the water. There were no lights burning then though they kept alight practically until the last. Before reaching the perpendicular when at an angle of 50 or 60 degrees, there was a rumbling sound which may be attributed to the boilers leaving their beds and crashing down on to or through the bulkheads. She became more perpendicular when she went slowly down. After sinking as far as the after part of the boat deck she went down more quickly. The ship disappeared at 2.20 a.m. *Mersey Report on the Loss of the Steamship Titanic*, 1912

The survivors in the lifeboats were picked up by the Cunard liner *Carpathia*, which was bound to Liverpool from New York when the *Titanic*'s CQD call was received at 12.25 a.m. Captain Rostron immediately turned his ship and steamed at her highest speed (17.5 knots) in the direction of *Titanic* fifty-eight miles away. About 2.40 a.m. he saw a green flare, which had been sent up by Mr Boxall in No. 2 lifeboat. At the same time ice was sighted and Captain Rostron, steaming at speed, had continually to alter course to avoid icebergs, while making for *Titanic*'s last position. At 4.10 a.m., just at daylight, the first lifeboat (No. 2) was picked up by *Carpathia*. The remaining lifeboats were scattered over an area of four to five miles and it was 8.00 a.m. before they had all been picked up. From these boats Captain Rostron took on board *Carpathia* 712 survivors, one of whom died shortly afterwards. This number saved represented 32 per cent of the total number of people on board *Titanic*. At the scene of the disaster there were only a few deckchairs, cork lifebelts and one body floating in the water.

THE UNSINKABLE SHIP?

Harland & Wolff did not claim that *Olympic* and *Titanic* were unsinkable. No shipbuilder would be so foolish. Great stress was however laid on the safety arrangements of the ships. Both *Olympic* and *Titanic* were built with double bottoms and their hulls were divided into sixteen virtually watertight compartments. They were designed to remain afloat with any two of these compartments flooded. *Titanic*'s collision with the iceberg was a freak accident in which six compartments were immediately open to the sea. It was impossible for the ship to remain afloat with such exceptional and unforeseen damage.

The idea of *Titanic* being an unsinkable ship probably derived from White Star's own publicity. The Line claimed that the Captain on the bridge could 'by simply moving an electric switch, instantly close the watertight doors throughout, practically making the vessel unsinkable'.

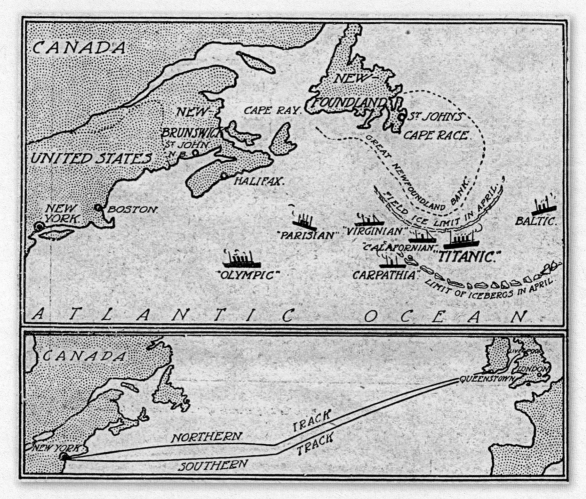

∧ 'The map shows the position of the icebergs on which Titanic struck, with the other liners that hurried to her assistance. She was following the southern or winter track, as shown on the smaller map. The northern track is only followed in summer months when the ocean is free of ice.' *The Deathless Story of the Titanic*, 1912.

THE QUESTION OF LIFEBOATS

Titanic's twenty lifeboats were in excess of Board of Trade rules, which required her to carry only sixteen boats. In 1912 lifeboat regulations did not relate to the number of people on board but to the tonnage of the ship. However, even these regulations were badly out of date, being the same for a ship of 10,000 tons as for *Titanic* at 46,000 tons.

Although *Titanic*'s type of Welin davits permitted the fitting of up to forty-eight lifeboats, enough for all on board, sufficient numbers of boats were not carried. It is likely that this was a White Star marketing decision. The additional boats would have interfered with the promenading space on the boat deck and reduced the sense of passenger safety that White Star was so anxious to promote.

At the time, consideration of safety at sea principally related to improvements in ship design, rather than to the complementary need for adequate lifeboat provision. It was only after the *Titanic* disaster that the idea of lifeboat space for everyone on board became accepted and enforced practice.

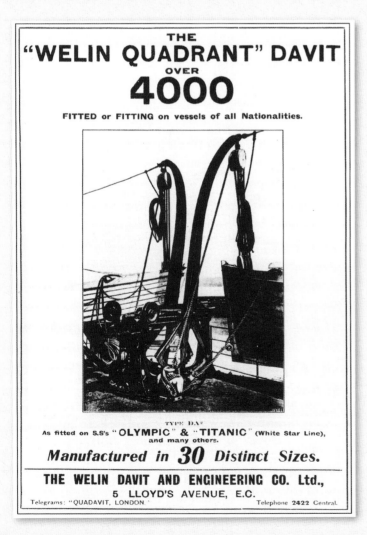

‹ Advertisement for the Welin-type davit, as fitted to *Titanic* for only sixteen lifeboats on the boat deck. The complacent failure by owners, builders and regulators to make sufficient lifeboat provision for all on board was at the heart of the *Titanic* disaster.

Titanic survivors in one of the lifeboats alongside the rescue ship Carpathia. Captain Rostron arrived at the scene of the disaster at 4.10 a.m. after navigating through the ice at high speed. All of Titanic's scattered lifeboats were picked up by 8.00 a.m.

Scene on board the rescue ship Carpathia steaming to New York. Women passengers are working to provide clothes for the Titanic survivors.

A trio of Titanic survivors on board Carpathia. Mr and Mrs George A. Harder were a honeymoon couple. He was the only man saved out of eleven honeymoon couples sailing in Titanic. To the right is Mrs Charles M. Hays, who lost her husband, the President of the Grand Trunk Railway.

AFTERMATH

The catastrophe had a traumatic impact on the British and American public. The impossible had happened and the ship 'representing the highest attainments in naval architecture and marine engineering' was lying two miles down on the bottom of the Atlantic. More than 1,500 people – passengers and crew – had gone down with her. As survivors began to tell their stories and the facts became known, every conceivable aspect of the disaster was documented and debated. Scapegoats were found and heroism acclaimed. The obeyed commands 'Be British' and 'Women and children first' struck patriotic chords. Captain Smith was widely believed to have rescued a child before he perished with his ship. The wireless operators had stayed at their posts to the end, as had the engineers and the ship's band. It was reported that the band had played 'Nearer, My God, to Thee' as *Titanic* went down. The sheet music became a bestseller and entrepreneurs, catching the mood of emotion, flooded a ready market with *Titanic* mementoes.

The cultural response to the sinking of *Titanic* was a remarkable phenomenon. Overwhelmingly it was popular and vernacular, but artists and writers also expressed the catastrophic event in terms of their individual imagination and vision of humanity. For the novelist and poet Thomas Hardy, the destruction of *Titanic* was a dramatic confirmation of his view that man existed at the whim of nature. The collision of ship and iceberg precisely reflected Hardy's sense of an 'ironic will' governing a universe where man was the victim of destiny rather than its master. His poem 'The Convergence of the Twain' was a powerful working of this theme:

> ... And as the smart ship grew
> In stature, grace, and hue,
> In shadowy silent distance
> grew the Iceberg too.
>
> Alien they seemed to be:
> No mortal eye could see
> The intimate welding
> of their later history.

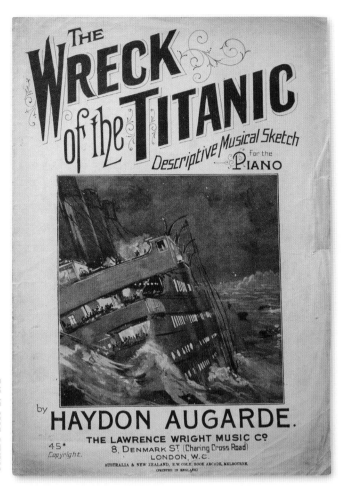

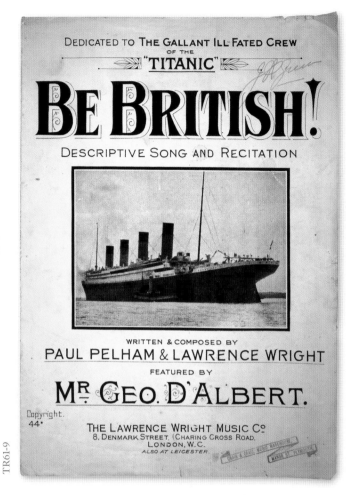

In Belfast, news of *Titanic*'s sinking was received with shock and grief, not only for the loss of the ship but because of the news that Thomas Andrews and a team of Harland & Wolff workers had perished with her. They were: William Parr, assistant manager, electrical department; Roderick Chisholm, ships' draughtsman; Anthony Frost, outside fireman engineer; Robert Knight, leading hand engineer; William Campbell, joiner apprentice; Alfred Cunningham, apprentice fitter; Frank Parkes, apprentice plumber and Ennis Watson, apprentice electrician.

After the collision it was Thomas Andrews who had first recognised that damage to *Titanic* was fatal. His professionalism, self-sacrifice and heroic attempts to save life were succinctly described in a telegram from White Star's New York offices:

> After accident Andrews ascertained damage, advised passengers put heavy clothing, prepare leave vessel. Many sceptical about seriousness damage, but impressed by Andrews' knowledge, personality, followed his advice, saved their lives. He assisted many women, children to lifeboats. When last seen, officers say was throwing overboard deck chairs, other objects to people in water. His chief concern safety of everyone but himself.

As a mark of respect to Thomas Andrews and the workmen who had lost their lives in the disaster, Harland & Wolff closed the shipyard on Saturday 20 April.

The men of Queen's Island were profoundly shaken by the catastrophe, especially as so many of them had been engaged in the construction of *Titanic*. An anonymous shipyard poet expressed the widespread sense of personal bereavement in the elegiac 'Big Boat 401':

> ... In a shipyard we're all workmates,
> No matter what our state,
> For a falling plank has no respect,
> When sealing a man's fate.
> That ship was flesh and bone of us;
> We loved her, and with pride
> We admire the men and women
> Who like heroes on her died.

On 22 April 1912, a week after the *Titanic* disaster, a journalist on the *Belfast News-Letter* reflected on the mood of sadness prevailing at Queen's Island:

> The loss of the vessel would itself have been a tremendous shock to them, but as compared with the tragic end of the men who were so recently moving about them full of life and vigour it is now felt to be of minor importance. A new *Titanic* as beautiful and stately as the ship which now lies at the bottom of the Atlantic can be built. The industry and resources of Belfast are equal to such a task as that; but none of the precious lives which have been lost can ever be restored or adequately compensated for. It is this feeling of irreparable loss which has caused a gloom to settle over the great shipbuilding yard in which the *Titanic* had her birth and neither time nor achievement can dispel the memory of the catastrophe or heal the grief that has taken possession of the hearts of men.

THE TITANIC SUNK.

COLLISION WITH ICEBERG.

1,500 LIVES LOST.

WIRELESS CALLS FOR HELP

LINERS TO THE RESCUE.

The maiden voyage of the new White Star liner Titanic ended in disaster yesterday morning, the giant vessel sinking, with about 1,500 of those on board, off the coast of Newfoundland, after collision with an iceberg.

The news of the collision was received on the night of the 14th inst. in Montreal by wireless telegraphy, and several Atlantic liners also picked up the Titanic's messages calling for immediate assistance.

The Virginian, Parisian, Baltic, Olympic, and other vessels proceeded at full speed to the damaged liner, and over 600 of the passengers were subsequently transferred without mishap. It is officially stated that many lives have been lost.

The passengers are being conveyed to Halifax, Nova Scotia, where they are due to arrive to-morrow, and preparations are being made for their conveyance to New York.

FROM OUR OWN CORRESPONDENT.

New York, Monday.

Late last night the White Star liner Titanic, on her maiden voyage from Southampton to New York, collided with an iceberg in latitude 41.46 degrees north, longitude 50.14 degrees west. This is the season of the year at which the southward drift of the icebergs calls for in——

was standing by, and that the White Star liner Baltic was approaching.

Presently the Virginian also arrived, and while the remainder of the passengers were being transferred to the Parisian, the Virginian got ready to attempt the difficult task of towing the Titanic into Halifax. The Titanic by this time was low in the water, and her foreholds were full, but ——

THE NEWS IN ——

Dramatic Midnight ——

NAMES OF SOME OF THE PASSENGERS.

FROM OUR OWN CORRESPONDENT.

New York, Monday.

The news of the disaster reached New York in the small hours of the morning by way of Montreal, whither it had been transmitted by wireless telegraphy from the Allan liner Virginian, eastward bound. The Virginian herself, in common with other liners whose names are household words in two Continents, had picked up in the night the wireless signals for assistance, sent broadcast by the maimed liner; and at the same moment that she was passing them on to the shore was steaming the fastest to the rescue. The excitement and dismay which the tidings aroused here may easily be imagined. New York was preparing to give the Titanic a big welcome on the same lines as that extended last year to her sister ship, the Olympic, and among her passengers, it was known, there were many distinguished American citizens, concerning whose fate the earlier message said nothing. Most of these, after fulfilling business and other engagements in Europe, had waited in order to enjoy the thrill of making the homeward journey in the world's greatest liner, the "millionaire's ship," on board which they might almost be pardoned for considering themselves as safe as in their hotels on shore. Among them may be mentioned the following:—

Mr. Benjamin Guggenheim, a member of the famous Guggenheim family of capitalists, associates of Mr. Pierpont Morgan, and world famous in connection with Alaskan development and copper production.

Mr. Clarence Jones, a New York stockbroker, who has been visiting European capitals in connection with the purchase of American Embassy sites.

Mr. Washington Roebling, head of the great wire cable firm and son of the builder of the Brooklyn Bridge.

Mr. Washington Dodge, member of the well-known banking firm of Phelps, Dodge, & Co.

Colonel John Weir, mining engineer.

Mr. Henry B. Harris, theatrical producer and manager and son of the gentleman of New York's theatres.

Mr. Jacques Futrelle, one of the best known of American authors.

Mr. Frank D. Millet, American painter, who resided a long time in London.

The publication of the Montreal message sent scores of anxious folk to the White Star offices here in quest of further information, but there was nothing to tell them for several long hours ——

RECEPTION OF THE —— IN BELFAST.

General Feeling of Regret.

LOCAL PASSENGERS AND SAILORS ON BOARD.

Nowhere has the news of the mishap to the Titanic been received with more sincere regret than in Belfast—the birthplace of the huge vessel—and fuller details concerning the accident are eagerly awaited. Like all the fleet of the White Star Line, she was built by Messrs. Harland & Wolff, Ltd., at the Queen's Island Shipbuilding Works, and the construction of the world's biggest ship, like that of her immediate predecessor and sister ship, the Olympic, was followed with the keenest interest by the community generally. It will be remembered that she was launched on Wednesday, the 31st May, 1911, and the ceremony was witnessed by many thousands of spectators, including several who had come across the channel to be present at the scene, which was certainly an impressive one. The vessel has been so fully and so recently described in our columns that it is unnecessary to repeat details which are already familiar to our readers, but it may be said that she represents the very latest ideas not only in regard to construction, but also in the matter of equipment, and that she cost close on two millions sterling. There was no public inspection prior to her departure from Belfast, but those who were specially privileged to make a tour through the great ship after her completion were deeply impressed by the immense size of the Titanic, as well as by the general excellence of her accommodation—special attention being attracted by the magnificent suite of rooms for millionaires and other wealthy passengers. The Titanic left Belfast on the morning of Tuesday, the 2nd inst., just a fortnight ago to-day, and proceeded to Southampton in order to take her place in the Atlantic service. On her departure she was accompanied by the best wishes of the citizens, and none of those who watched her slowly gliding down the harbour and the lough anticipated that her maiden voyage would have such a disastrous ending. Her sailing from Belfast had been delayed for a day by the tempestuous weather and the heavy seas prevailing, but the conditions on the morning of her actual departure were highly favourable, and, like the Olympic, she steamed away amid brilliant sunshine. She reached Southampton on the night of the 3rd inst., and left that port on her maiden voyage on Wednesday last, 10th inst.

Amongst those on board the ill-fated liner at the time of the disaster was Mr. Thomas Andrews, jun., one of the directors of Messrs. Harland & Wolff, Limited. It is highly probable that Lord Pirrie, K.P., chairman of the firm, would, in accordance with his usual custom, have been on board, as the representative of the builders, had it not been for the serious illness which confined him to his bed, but from which he is now ——

Belfast News-Letter, 16 April 1912

Belfast Evening Telegraph, 16 April 1912

TITANIC LOST

Unparalleled Shipping Calamity

TRAGIC COLLAPSE OF A MAIDEN VOYAGE

REPORTED LOSS OF OVER 1,600 LIVES.

WOMEN AND CHILDREN SAVED.

675 Rescued by Lifeboats.

GRAPHIC DETAILS.

This coloured lantern ❯ slide dramatically depicts the lowering of one of *Titanic*'s lifeboats filled with women and children, as men remain behind. The popular messages that came out of the disaster were self-sacrifice, heroism, duty and stoicism in the face of death. (OMAFP-2010-27-530/5)

In 1912 there was no ❯ visual record of the *Titanic* disaster as it unfolded. This coloured lantern slide, drawn after the event, is a vivid depiction of the horror of the night. Viewed from the safety of the lifeboats, hundreds of people have been left behind to perish on board the sinking ship. (OMAFP-2010-27-530/7)

In Memoriam

"TITANIC"

SUNK ON HER MAIDEN VOYAGE OFF CAPE RACE, APRIL 15th, 1912.

The most appalling disaster in Maritime History, with a loss of over 1,500 lives.

Titanic disaster memento. In spite of the name shown on the bow, this ship is not *Titanic*, but her sister ship *Olympic*, of which more photographs were available at that time. (BR96)

"NEARER MY GOD TO THEE."

PHOTOGRAPHS AND PHOTOGRAPHERS

Since the invention of photography over 170 years ago, photographs have become a most important source of visual information about the past. They help us to understand better the times to which they belonged, through their delineation of reality and accuracy of description. However, as with all types of evidence, historic photographs should be considered critically and interpreted in the light of other knowledge. Although photographs cannot explain the factors which shaped the events of their day, their appeal has always been the capacity to show and preserve the appearance of things at a precise point in time. With their layered imagery, they are unique and often evocative visual records of events, people, places and things which can never be brought together in the same way again. As authentic records of existence, photographs touch our sense of mortality by becoming markers of time's passage and signifiers of the transience of life.

Views of maritime activity in Belfast were amongst the first outdoor photographs taken in Britain or Ireland. Using the daguerreotype process, Francis S. Beatty, a well-known local engraver and photographic pioneer, recorded quayside shipping near the Old Long Bridge in August 1840. Alas these photographs (daguerreotypes) have not survived and indeed relatively few maritime photographs predate the 1880s. From this date onwards photography became cheaper, simpler and hence more popular. New processes, materials and equipment permitted greater mobility and allowed shorter exposure times, so not only did the number of photographers and photographs increase, but the range of pictures also became more varied. Henceforward it was possible for photographers to record virtually every aspect of the world in which they lived.

Thousands of photographs were taken at home, in the country and in the streets; people were photographed in studios, on holiday, at leisure and at work. By the early twentieth century, photographers, reflecting contemporary pride in the progress of technology and invention, were recording the latest engineering achievements, from motor cars to aeroplanes, from electric trams to ocean liners.

The photographs in this book have been selected from images in the extensive Photographic Archive of the Ulster Folk and Transport Museum, National Museums Northern Ireland. Most of them belong to major collections of glass-plate negatives, but others have been taken from old prints loaned or donated to the museum in albums or as individual photographs. The key images of *Titanic* and shipbuilding at Belfast are drawn from the Archive's Harland & Wolff Photographic Collection. Comprising some 75,000 negatives, it provides a remarkable visual record of the development of the world-famous shipbuilding firm of Harland & Wolff from the mid-1890s to almost the present day. As a specialist photographic collection, it is of international significance because it depicts the changing output and infrastructure of a shipbuilding company that has always been,

R.J. Welch, Harland & Wolff's official photographer, was photographed by fellow photographer W.A. Green on 1 April 1911, while recording the docking of *Olympic* – the world's largest ship – in the largest drydock in the world. (WAG 3196)

and continues to be, at the leading edge of naval architecture and marine technology. The *Titanic* photographs in the Harland & Wolff collection, together with *Titanic* images from other sources, have established the museum's Photographic Archive as holding, probably, the world's largest and most important collection of *Titanic* photographic negatives.

Prior to the early 1920s, when Harland & Wolff established its own permanent photographic department, the majority of shipyard photographs were taken by the well-known Belfast professional photographer R.J. Welch (1859–1936). From the mid-1890s to the First World War he had a regular commission to photograph industrial progress and achievement at Queen's Island. Welch's photographs form an outstanding record of shipyard plant and production during this period. Often taken in the most difficult circumstances, these photographs, with their great depth of field and carefully selected viewpoints, are models of industrial photography. They set high standards for later photographers working with more sophisticated equipment and materials. R.J. Welch shared Harland & Wolff's pride in the extensive shipbuilding enterprise at Queen's Island and was determined to make his photographs 'the best possible record for the benefit of future generations'.

Mention should be made of another professional photographer, W.A. Green (1870–1958), whose work is also reproduced in the preceding pages. The museum's W. A. Green Collection of almost 4,000 glass-plate negatives dates from *c.*1910–1935. It is a core source of visual information about urban and rural life during this period. Although many of Green's photographs were taken for commercial purposes, and the subjects often carefully arranged, his documentary work characteristically implies relationships between past and present, tradition and modernity, in the people and the places of his native land.

The photographs of *Titanic* and the times in which she was built bear haunting witness to an irrecoverable past. But these images also embody paradox and ambiguity. Like all documentary photographs they claim precision of record, but often the imagery is puzzling and we cannot know or understand all that is being disclosed. However, as visual quotations from fragmented history, they invite us to reflect with empathy on the past and connect it imaginatively with the present.

National Museums Northern Ireland brings the timeless tale of the *Titanic* to life through TITANICa at the Ulster Folk & Transport Museum. Discover more than 500 original artefacts including original ship plans produced in Harland & Wolff's drawing office over 100 years ago. Get close to *Titanic* with these real objects from her world. Walk the historic streets and meet the people who lived in her time.

National Museums Northern Ireland's website, www.nmni.com, provides detailed information on *Titanic*-related collections including photographs, artefacts and art.

Prints of photographs reproduced in this book along with an extensive collection of historical and art images are available to purchase from National Museums Northern Ireland's Picture Library by visiting www.nmni.com/picturelibrary.

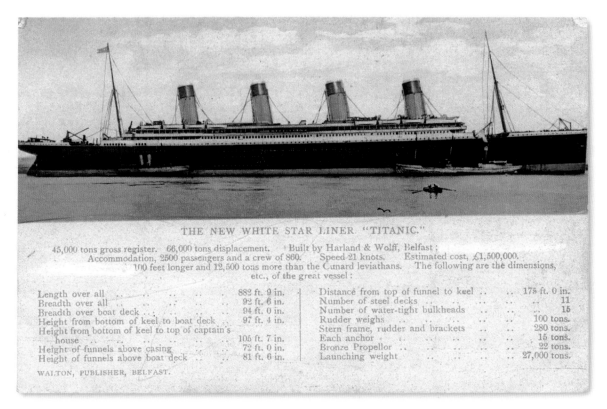

THE NEW WHITE STAR LINER "TITANIC."

45,000 tons gross register. 66,000 tons displacement. Built by Harland & Wolff, Belfast; Accommodation, 2500 passengers and a crew of 860. Speed 21 knots. Estimated cost, £1,500,000. 100 feet longer and 12,500 tons more than the Cunard leviathans. The following are the dimensions, etc., of the great vessel :

Length over all	882 ft. 9 in.	Distance from top of funnel to keel	175 ft. 0 in.
Breadth over all	92 ft. 6 in.	Number of steel decks	11
Breadth over boat deck	94 ft. 0 in.	Number of water-tight bulkheads	15
Height from bottom of keel to boat deck	97 ft. 4 in.	Rudder weighs	100 tons.
Height from bottom of keel to top of captain's house	105 ft. 7 in.	Stern frame, rudder and brackets	280 tons.
		Each anchor	15 tons.
Height of funnels above casing	72 ft. 0 in.	Bronze Propellor	22 tons.
Height of funnels above boat deck	81 ft. 6 in.	Launching weight	27,000 tons.

WALTON, PUBLISHER, BELFAST.

△ Rare colour postcard of *Titanic*
  fitting out in Belfast.

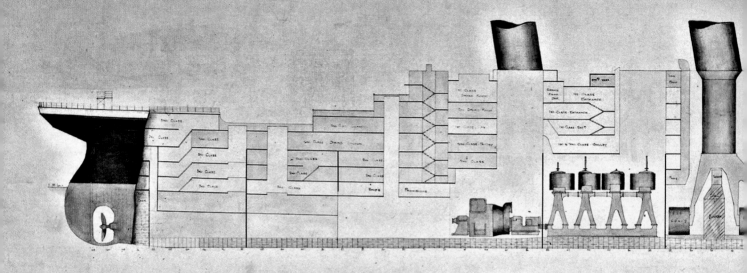

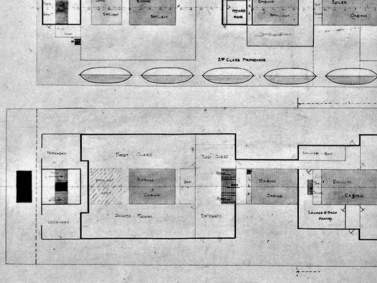

Original design drawings for *Olympic*
and *Titanic*, prepared by Harland &
Wolff and approved in Belfast on 29
July 1908 by Bruce Ismay and other
White Star Line directors. (TR138-8)

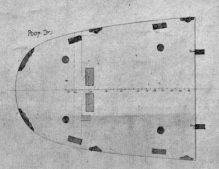

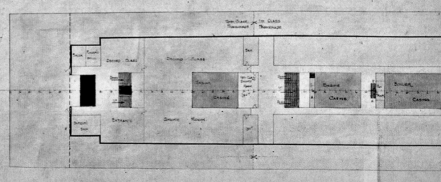